Quick

"Patrick Adams contrasts the cultures of two companies he worked for and though each started with similar lean models and visions one was mechanistic and only gave the appearance of lean, while the other developed an actual culture of continuous improvement. The contrast provides a vivid example of the difference between fake lean and true lean."

~ Dr. Jeffrey K. Liker, Author of *The Toyota Way*

"So many companies appear to be Lean but in reality haven't scratched the surface of a truly Lean culture. Patrick gives you an opportunity to consider your own leadership journey with thought provoking questions throughout the book based on his own personal experiences. The real life stories of the two companies portrayed in this book, like the 'perfect storm' example inside Company Continuous Appearance – vs. the example of True North at Company Continuous Improvement will help you see the gaps which exist in your company. The 12 questions, recommended by Patrick Adams in this book will help any reader assess their organization as it pertains to a Lean culture. This book is a must-read for anyone with interest in moving toward a "real" daily improvement culture."

~ Charlie Protzman, Shingo-Prize Winning Author

"Avoiding the Continuous Appearance Trap is practical guide to a better understanding of your organization's operations. Reflecting on your own answers to Adams' 12 questions will reveal breadth and depth of your current state that you had most likely never known. Like most aspects of Lean, this is a simple concept that leads to transformative results."

~ Steven Kane, Gemba Academy LLC

"Many organizations attempt to apply continuous improvement tools as ends in themselves rather than means to a higher purpose. In his engaging new book, Avoiding The Continuous Appearance Trap, Patrick Adams likens such a rudderless approach to "putting lipstick on a pig." At a distance there may be a likeness to continuous improvement, but closer inspection unmasks a façade of Lean artifacts that look good for customer tours but are otherwise purposeless and even counterproductive. For any continuous improvement leader charged with transforming his or her organization from status quo to world-class, Adams book poses twelve critical questions you should be prepared to answer. His empathetic narrative of two hypothetical organizations, "Company Continuous Improvement" and "Company Continuous Appearance" illustrates the consequences of differing answers to each of these questions. A good read for improvement leaders that are either just getting started or have been struggling for some time without results."

~ **Bruce Hamilton, President of GBMP**

"In today's culture, we're all familiar with the term 'fake news,' but there's also something called 'fake lean.' Patrick Adams lays out, in a very succinct way, the telltale signs of authentically lean and fake lean. There couldn't be a better analysis for all of us to make sure we're not posers but our efforts are the real thing."

~ **Paul Akers, Author of *2 Second Lean***

Free Assessment Download

Go to: www.avoidcontinuousappearance.com

and download your free assessment today!

Get in Contact:

office@findleansolutions.com

Find, Follow, and Share on Social Media:

- @PatrickAdamsii
- @FindingLeanSolutions
- @pa.consulting

AVOIDING THE *CONTINUOUS* APPEARANCE TRAP

12 questions to understand what's truly underneath your culture.

Patrick Adams

First edition published in 2021

By Patrick Adams Consulting Services, LLC

Copyright © 2021 by Patrick Adams Consulting Services, LLC

This book contains information obtained from authentic and highly regarded sources. Reasonable efforts have been made to publish reliable data and information, but the author and publisher cannot assume responsibility for the validity of all materials or the consequences of their use. The author and publisher have attempted to trace the copyright holders of all material reproduced in this publication and apologize to copyright holders if permission to publish in this form have not been obtained. If any copyright material has not been acknowledged please write and let us know so we can rectify in any future reprint.

Except as permitted under U.S. Copyright Law, no part of this book may be reprinted, reproduced, transmitted, or utilized in any form by electronic, mechanical, or other means, now known or hereafter invented, including photocopying, microfilming, and recording, or in any information storage or retrieval system, without written permission from the publisher.

Editing by: Jim Vinoski, Kara Levy

ISBN: 978-1-7361309-0-2

Library of Congress Control Number: 2020925940

Created in the United States of America

www.findleansolutions.com

www.avoidcontinuousappearance.com

office@findleansolutions.com

*This book is dedicated to my first lean coach,
Dave Remus, and the relentless and unwavering
commitment he made to my personal
development as a leader, lean practitioner, and coach.
Dave passed away, unexpectedly,
on December 28th, 2019.*

ACKNOWLEDGEMENTS

I would like to thank all my clients for their contributions to the development of the assessment and recommendations for change you will find throughout this book. I would also like to thank those I worked with at both the Company of Continuous Improvement and the Company of Continuous Appearance for the many lessons I will share throughout this book.

A special thanks to Robert Heath Sr., Heidi Peterson, and Stephen Sweers.

CONTENTS

Foreword..1

Introduction..9

Meet the Team...21

1 Are You Content?...37

2 Where Are Your Leaders Spending Their Time?...........51

3 Are You Pursuing Perfection?..............................67

4 How Stable Are You Today?................................83

5 Who's Accountable?...95

6 What Are Your Goals?......................................107

7 Is Your Organization Designed to Meet Your Goals?...119

8 How Are Your Leaders Behaving?.....................131

9 How Safe Is It For Your Employees To Fail?......145

10 What Is Your High Value Target Area?............159

11 Are You Generating Small, Simple Improvements?...169

12 Are Problems Easy To See?.............................179

Conclusion...189

Assessment...199

About the Author..207

Foreword

I met Patrick Adams for the first time in the summer of 2019 when he signed up for my newly-announced Japan Study Trip for the following spring of 2020. Patrick's passion and enthusiasm for connecting with people, developing himself as a learner and leader, and helping others succeed was evident from our first conversation. And in the following eighteen months since our first meeting, I've come to know and deeply appreciate Patrick's approach to leadership and learning, and his commitment to helping others.

Patrick embodies the spirit of the motto that Isao Yoshino, a 40-year Toyota leader, and I adopted through our partnership in developing the book *Learning to Lead, Leading to Learn: Lessons from Toyota Leader Isao Yoshino on a Lifetime of Continuous Learning*: 1 + 1 = much more than 2. To me, this means the sum of people working together is much more than what any of us can accomplish on our own. Patrick's commitment to supporting others in achieving their best selves is evident in all that he does, from helping leaders at all levels learn how to lead with a learning mindset and how to achieve

FOREWORD

business results while developing people at the same time, to seeing himself as a consummate learner too.

I've spent years working in and with companies striving to develop a people-centered learning culture founded on lean principles, through studying the practices of successful lean companies in Japan and around the world. In my experience, too many companies and their leaders focus on the visible artifacts of continuous improvement without understanding the underlying principles and the actions they as leaders need to take to create a culture of continuous improvement: to set direction, provide support, and develop themselves as leaders at the same time.

As I learned from Isao Yoshino, over years of conversation that resulted in the book *Learning to Lead, Leading to Learn*, the only secret to Toyota — the model for what has become known as lean — is its secret towards learning. It is their organizational focus on developing people first, and creating a culture that embraces the process of learning through failure and success, that differentiates them from their competitors and those who wish to emulate Toyota's success.

This attitude towards learning and people development is what companies with real cultures of continuous improvement get right. Getting it wrong is the crux of what keeps many companies stuck in a cycle of what Patrick describes as continuous appearance — one focused on the external artifacts and tools of improvement but not the underlying foundation of learning and people development.

What awaits you on the pages that follow is more than a how-to book for creating a culture of continuous improvement in your organization. In *Avoiding the Continuous Appearance Trap*, Patrick offers you his real-life learning experiences about what it takes to move from a culture of continuous appearance to one that embodies an authentic people-centered learning culture of continuous improvement. The messages within *Avoiding the Continuous Appearance Trap* are important for leaders at all levels — whether you are an individual contributor, an emerging leader, or an established leader — in any industry.

We all learn best through stories and in *Avoiding the Continuous Appearance Trap*, Patrick brings twelve foundational practices of continuous improvement culture to light through contrasting case studies of two different organizations that he worked in early in his career.

As you will discover on the pages that follow, one of the companies had a true culture of continuous improvement, where leaders led with a focus on developing people in service of making products. In contrast, the other company had what Patrick calls a culture of continuous appearance. Underneath all the floor tape, the fancy visual scorecards, and posters professing "The Lean Mindset" or "5S To Success," was an organization focused on output at the expense of its people, resulting in high turnover rates and subpar performance.

If you were to walk into either of these companies, they would look very similar. Both had similar organizational structures and operational metrics (or key performance indicators —KPIs) of safety, quality, cost, and delivery defined and visually displayed on the walls of the factory. From just an outside glimpse, it would be hard for you to determine differences in their approach to business solutions. However, when looking underneath the visible artifacts of improvement and continuous improvement tools, you'd see that the two companies were vastly different.

Through Patrick's real-life experiences in these two companies, you can see the impact of leaders' choices and actions on a company's culture and outcomes.

In Company Continuous Improvement, leaders at all levels understood both their purpose as people-centered leaders and the actions they needed to take to align with and fulfill that purpose. As you will discover, the leaders were not perfect by any means, but they saw mistakes and failure as a source for learning and improvement, and took steps to demonstrate that they put their people and learning

FOREWORD

at the forefront of their priorities. They took steps to align their actions in the direction of the culture of continuous improvement they wanted to build each and every day.

In contrast, at Company Continuous Appearance, leaders lacked awareness of how their actions were not aligned with their professed purpose and values. For example, you will learn in the introduction of *Avoiding the Continuous Appearance Trap* that the plant manager, Chris, loved the idea of being a leader who builds a team and develops his people. However, his actions did not align with this desire. He found it easier to delegate and to stay in his office, and did not accept any form of failure from anyone on the team, often yelling at team members if they failed. His actions created a culture of fear and disengagement across the company.

Through the twelve chapters of this book, Patrick gives you an opportunity to consider your own leadership journey with thought-provoking questions. He describes the importance of the principle of continuous improvement underlying each question, and offers you real examples of how you can apply all the principles so that you can create a culture of continuous improvement, not continuous appearance.

Continuous improvement is a journey towards excellence, but one without a final destination.

The process of learning is never over and is never complete. Similarly, as you read each of the chapters covering the twelve questions in *Avoiding the Continuous Appearance Trap*, learn from Patrick's stories and reflect on your own experiences. Use the questions as a catalyst for your own personal improvement, and identify how you can create a culture of real continuous improvement in your organization, one person at a time.

Take a moment to identify what kind of leader you want to be and the culture that you want in your organization. Use the questions posed at the end of each of the twelve chapters on the pages that follow to identify the actions you need to take to be that leader and to create that type of culture. And then take steps to bring these actions into your daily practice and learn by doing, and day by day fulfill your purpose as a leader who enables an authentic continuous improvement culture.

Katie Anderson, Author of *Learning to Lead, Leading to Learn*

December 2020

Introduction

As a young production supervisor, I wanted to prove myself to upper management. I saw others getting promoted into high-paying positions and thought if only I could make a good impression early on, then I too could one day sit in a corner office with a window.

But how would I do it?

I needed to learn what was important to the management team and the executives. So, whenever I saw the front-office door open, I would meet the managers and offer a tour. As I walked the production floor with them, I watched when their eyes lit up and listened for excitement in their voices. I learned what wowed them and what did not.

Here was my takeaway: Most importantly, the managers never wanted to hear that my team had missed a shipment, no matter what. Outside of that, they seemed pretty easy to please. But there were a few things that seemed to grab their attention. They liked to see clean, well-lit work areas with fresh paint. They smiled when they saw visual boards with charts and improvement activities; however, the charts needed

INTRODUCTION

to have lots of green key performance indicators (KPIs)...never red! Finally, I learned they always showed interest when teams had new improvements to show off to them.

Knowing this, I got to work and began to play the part. I received approval to paint a few machines and upgrade the lighting in my area. I purchased a whiteboard and posted some charts from the front office. I added one chart to track the teams' output, and I made sure the goal was easy enough that we were always in the green. Finally, I added a section for a task list to show how busy the team was with improvement projects. I printed some motivational posters I found on the Web with words I knew the front office executives would be impressed with like "5S*" and "Leadership." I even posted a daily safety message and a quote of the day in my area.

I stopped spending time on the production floor because I wanted upper management to see more of me in the management meetings. When my team tried to ask for help, I told them to figure it out on their own but then always accepted the kudos from upper management when things worked out in my favor. I even went as far as to reprimand my team when the charts were not updated with fake information prior to an executive tour.

I felt proud of the "new" department. I even took before-and-after pictures and emailed them to the management team. Then I waited, knowing they would soon want to come see all the great work happening in my area.

I was ready for that promotion. I pictured myself sitting in the comfortable office chair up front within the next few weeks.

When the time finally came for an executive visit and management walk-about, I left my dirty jeans and t-shirt at home and replaced them with dress slacks and a collared shirt. I was clean-shaven and even

---

* 5S refers to a system by which our workplace is organized. 5S provides an on-going self-regulated system that instills a discipline to create, improve, and maintain a clean and well-organized, work environment.

AVOIDING THE CONTINUOUS APPEARANCE TRAP

sprayed on my best cologne. I shut down the machines for a few hours and directed my employees to clean up. I told them how important it was to put on a good show!

While the executives were impressed that day, I didn't receive that promotion I had hoped for. You see, my team missed shipments that day and many days after. My employees saw through my false intentions and knew I really didn't respect them. It was clear to them that I was here for myself and not the team. This became even more clear when I removed the tools they needed for production because I felt they made the area look cluttered. How would they do their jobs without the proper tools? I didn't care as long as it made me look good in front of the executives.

There's an old saying: You can put lipstick on a pig, but it's still a pig. In this case, I was the pig.

***

Does this sound familiar? So many companies struggle with leaders who say one thing but do another. Leaders appear to want positive change, but their actions reveal something very different. Luckily, I learned very quickly that this type of behavior creates a toxic environment where people hate to work, and I changed my entire approach. Slapping some paint on a machine is easy. However, real and lasting change is difficult and takes respect, dedication, and time.

Maybe your leaders aren't as bad as I was. I've grown a lot since those years as a young production supervisor and I've changed my ways considerably. However, maybe your leaders are much different than I was, and they are trying their best to carry out enough of the "right" improvement activities to make a difference.

Robert Schaffer and Harvey Thomson, authors of an article published in the Harvard Business Review[*], explain this phenomenon well:

> *"The performance improvement efforts of many companies*

---
[*] https://hbr.org/1992/01/successful-change-programs-begin-with-results

INTRODUCTION

have as much impact on operational and financial results as a ceremonial rain dance has on the weather. While some companies constantly improve measurable performance, in many others, managers continue to dance round and round the campfire – exuding faith and dissipating energy. This 'rain dance' is the ardent pursuit of activities that sound good, look good, and allow managers to feel good-but in fact contribute little or nothing to bottom-line performance. Companies introduce these programs under the false assumption that if they carry out enough of the 'right' improvement activities, actual performance improvements will inevitably materialize."

Organizations are allowing this cycle of improvement programs to persist, most times unknowingly, and the result is not a culture of continuous improvement. Rather, the result is what I like to call a "culture of continuous *appearance*." Cultures of continuous *appearance* appear to have it all together at the surface.

When it comes to certain strategies, methodologies, or programs, these companies appear to be doing the right thing. The walls are covered in leadership posters and improvement acronyms. The lunchroom tables have pretty informational postcards with constant reminders of how to identify waste and which behaviors provide the best results. Visual boards with metric charts can be found throughout the operation. Yellow tape on the floor signals proper locations for workstations and trash cans. However, behind all the good-looking charts and posters is a toxic culture struggling to stay afloat—a culture where leaders talk the talk, but don't walk the walk. A fear-based culture where the metric charts are always green because people are blamed every time red appears on a graph. Or the metric charts are not updated regularly at all because the team knows they don't mean anything. In these companies, leaders usually make all the decisions and do not share accountability. Mid-management to executive leadership is rarely visible to front-line workers, since they are usually busy in conference rooms or corner offices.

AVOIDING THE CONTINUOUS APPEARANCE TRAP

Organizations with a culture of continuous *appearance* are usually easy to identify due to their high turnover, mediocre metrics, low productivity, and low employee engagement. The only people who know what's really going on are those who work under the surface of these companies operating in a culture of continuous *appearance*.

But it doesn't have to be this way.

Whether your leaders are acting in ways similar to the way I was back then, or you find yourself in the "rain dance," if you don't like the results you're seeing—those metrics measured for organizational success—you must ask yourself: What is the biggest obstacle to boosting your numbers and making sure improvements stick?

The answer is culture.

This book will uncover the truth about your culture and how twelve simple questions can help you identify the culture you want. You'll start making decisions and supporting that culture by taking action and modeling a true culture of continuous improvement.

The framework for this book is going to be told through a comparison of two case studies, real examples, in which I had intimate experiences. These case studies represent two global companies similar in size and scope. These companies are similar at the surface, but, as you will discover, very

> **This book will uncover the truth about your culture and how twelve simple questions can help you identify the culture you want. You'll start making decisions and supporting that culture by taking action and modeling a true culture of continuous improvement.**

INTRODUCTION

different underneath.

Starting Our Case Study: Company Continuous Improvement vs. Company Continuous Appearance

I have been delivering bottom-line results through specialized process improvement solutions for over twenty years. Through my work as a Six Sigma Black Belt and Executive Lean Coach, I have trained thousands of successful change agents and have been actively involved with hundreds of organizations.

However, I've learned everything I know today through practical application, working in various companies in different industries. I have worked for all types of businesses from private, non-profit, government, and manufacturing, ranging from small businesses to billion-dollar corporations.

Early in my career, I had the opportunity to work for a few different manufacturing companies in operations management. Working as a production supervisor, operations manager, and plant manager gave me the operations and people skills necessary to deploy successful continuous improvement activities with leaders of other organizations. It also gave me experience working in many different working environments and working for leaders with different leadership styles. Those leadership styles were not too different than those I experienced during the eight years I served in the United States Marine Corps. Both allowed me to develop my skills in leadership and problem-solving, as well as my ability to adapt and overcome obstacles I would face later in life.

There were two organizations that stand out from those I have worked with all over the world. While both companies and the stories are very real, I have changed some minor details and will refer to each company with made-up names to protect those involved.

If you were to walk into either of these companies, at the surface they would look very similar. However, underneath they were very different.

The first company can be characterized by its amazing culture of continuous improvement. Let's call it, "Company Continuous Improvement." Company Continuous Improvement provides motion control solutions for the automotive industry, specializing in assembly, stamping, and tier-one supplier applications.

The second company can be characterized by its culture of continuous *appearance*. "Company Continuous Appearance" is a full service, tier-one automotive and industrial component supplier.

Both Company Continuous Appearance and Company Continuous Improvement determine current performance and establish goals for success by using the following KPIs: Safety, Quality, Cost, Delivery, and Morale. Both have adopted 'lean[*]' as their continuous improvement methodology. However, their approach, understanding, and deployment of lean to the organization is completely different. One approach is very successful and has proven bottom-line results, and the other is very detrimental to the organization.

In the following chapters, I will explain my experience in working for both organizations as an operations leader. I'll share what works and what doesn't when creating a culture of continuous improvement. My hope is that you will take my learning, especially that from Company Continuous Improvement, and establish a culture of continuous improvement within your own organization. Because every organization is different, you'll need to experiment with all the tools and techniques. Understand some will work and some will not; you may have to be flexible with the tools and techniques to make them work for your team. Feel free to adjust the approach or experiment with techniques you and your team create. At the end of the day, you will need to create your own way of doing things that works for your organization and solves problems specific to your operation.

---

[*] The term "Lean" was defined in 1996 by James Womack and Daniel Jones to consist of five key principles; 'Precisely specify value by specific product, identify the value stream for each product, make value flow without interruptions, let customer pull value from the producer, and pursue perfection.' (Womack and Jones 1996 p10)

INTRODUCTION

But be careful!

As you read through the twelve questions in this book, you may feel overwhelmed. You may ask yourself, "How could I possibly take all these actions to achieve the state I want?" Well, the good news is, not only do you not have to, but you shouldn't. Many of you will read this book and agree you have a culture of continuous appearance. If you understand the problem, recognize it, and can determine a countermeasure, your first inclination will be to go implement it. You will want to implement the proper answers to these questions right away in hopes of creating this culture of continuous improvement. However, you must be careful not to begin assigning action items to your team and sending them off to implement solutions you believe are laid out in this book. You will not fix much of anything.

Instead, try to assume you don't know what actions to take. In fact, you should try to prevent yourself from having any knowledge of action. Human behaviors and culture are complex and very complicated. If you want to have a chance at being successful, you must have a direction and a purpose and know why. You must break down the problem into smaller pieces and work on them one by one, overcoming obstacles and learning as you go.

I have included assessment questions at the end of each chapter with a combined assessment at the end of the book. Use your honest answers to guide you and determine where to begin.

This will become more of an evolutionary process of learning rather than an implementation process of correcting. I am not suggesting you can break down your culture into small pieces, but I am suggesting that your culture will emerge as a result of areas addressed with the questions laid out in this book. Examples include leadership behaviors, your approach to problem solving, organizational hierarchy, and others.

This is the beginning of scientific thinking for your organization. What is the value to you in reading about two case studies; one successful and one not successful? Under scientific thinking, the goal is for you to think about where you need to be in your situation, set a vision, develop a challenge, and then break the challenge down into smaller targets and go after them one by one, experimenting to overcome each obstacle. There is a great model for this in Mike Rother's Improvement Kata[*].

Mike Rother studied Toyota's management system and found practices and patterns of scientific thinking being used every day, with managers and mentors as the coaches. Toyota Kata is a skill-building process to shift our mindset and habits from a natural tendency to jump to conclusions to a tendency to think and work more scientifically. At a high level, Toyota Kata is a four-step pattern of moving from a current condition toward a desired future state by working iteratively (scientifically) through obstacles by learning from them and adapting based on what's being learned.

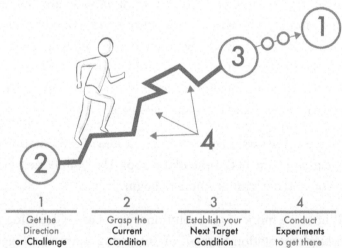

1	2	3	4
Get the Direction or Challenge	Grasp the Current Condition	Establish your Next Target Condition	Conduct Experiments to get there

By Mike Rother

In the following chapters, you will find case studies where I will talk about Company Continuous Improvement as the desired future state and Company Continuous Appearance as a current condition typical within companies who have adopted lean as their improvement

---
[*] For a detailed model of Improvement Kata, see Mike Rother, Toyota Kata (US: McGraw-Hill, 2009)

INTRODUCTION

methodology and struggled with results. You will also find a framework to guide you through twelve questions about your organization and those leadership behaviors happening inside your company.

The only way to change or transform your culture is by changing the leadership behaviors, and this must begin at the top. My recommendation is to work through these questions with your executive leadership team to help identify your current and desired state. Help leaders understand their impact on the system. From here, use the *Call To Action* at the end of each chapter along with the *Chapter Assessment Questions* to help determine your desired state and your current state in answering each question. This becomes your challenge. Once that is done, it's time to conduct experiments, remove obstacles, and begin the journey toward your desired state.

Let's dive in!

Meet the Team

Let's start by meeting the first company that I'll be comparing and contrasting through the book.

Company Continuous Improvement is based in a large booming city in the United States. Their manufacturing plants, however, are strategically placed in small farm communities in rural areas around the country. Company Continuous Improvement believes farmers and their families to be smart, innovative, scientifically-minded individuals each with an incredible work ethic, a uniquely confident humility, and a passion for their job that only comes with carrying on a family legacy. Based on my personal experience with them, they are spot on! By placing their manufacturing plants in these rural areas, they are filling their workforce ranks with the people that fit their ideal demographic.

Company Continuous Improvement is committed to standards and consistency. Every factory is set up to run on a similar system. Even though each factory makes completely different products, the look and feel inside the factories is very similar. Someone can walk in and go

MEET THE TEAM

directly to the factory visual site board. On the site board, they can identify the site metrics and quickly identify if and where any problems exist.

Let's imagine, in looking at the site board KPIs, we identify a problem: The team is not making its quality goal. From the site board, we would also be able to see which product line or area of the factory is contributing to the factory quality problem. From there, you can walk to that area of the factory and find a team improvement board. On the team improvement board, you will find a quality chart for that area being filled out daily by each shift. Here you will learn which product or machine is contributing to the problem and what the team is doing about it. There is active problem-solving shown on this board in response to the quality issue. The team members' actions are directly connected to the factory KPIs. They know what success looks like for their area and how they are personally contributing to the company's objectives.

In addition to this, someone can walk through the factory, and through various visual cues, they will know exactly what is going on without someone having to tell them. They will be able to tell you which machines are ahead or behind schedule. They can tell you what is supposed to be received in that day as well as what is shipping out. They can even show you what needed to be done and who would be notified if a line went down.

Here is the amazing part: While it is a large global company, someone can walk into a factory in Michigan and one in Poland, or wherever in the world, and see the exact same system in place and being followed!

One manufacturing site was placed sixty minutes north of the nearest major city in a small village with a population just under 1,000 people. A short drive around the area reveals nothing but corn and bean fields, Amish cheese, and cow pastures—exactly what Company Continuous Improvement preferred.

Dave

The plant manager, Dave, grew up just down the road from the factory and received his engineering degree from the city university. While serving in the United States Army, Dave traveled outside his home state for the first time in his life. He was a local, just like most of his team. Upon hiring in, Dave was immersed in Company Continuous Improvement's leadership development and training programs which started all the way at the top with the Vice President of Continuous Improvement and cascaded through the company to the front-line team members. Everything Dave learned, executive leaders and his team members had also learned. This was important because it meant they were "speaking the same language" when it came to problem solving and continuous improvement initiatives.

Dave never seemed to be content with anything. It didn't matter how smoothly a machine was running, Dave would be out on the production floor during his lunch time, with his sleeves rolled up, running his own experiments with team members to find ways to improve. Usually the experiments were in response to a problem one of the team members had expressed to Dave while he was out on one of his many daily walks through the factory. After many failed attempts to reduce the problem, eventually Dave and the team members would figure it out and find a solution that worked. Sometimes you could hear the cheers from across the factory. It wasn't every day, but the team members loved working alongside Dave. They learned to challenge the status quo and always look for ways to get better. They knew what they were accountable for and whether they had a successful day or not.

Dave led the daily factory meetings at the same time every day. The entire team was accountable for decisions made during that meeting. We always walked away with a clear understanding of the prior day's success or lack of success, and our actions for that day to ensure we ended every day successfully. During these meetings, our daily walks through the factory, and in regular conversations, Dave reminded us about our goals, both as a team and individually.

MEET THE TEAM

The Team

Scott and John worked together as managers reporting directly to Dave, while Claudette, Ed, and Randy served as supervisors on Dave's team. As I mentioned earlier, when faced with a problem, the entire team spoke the same universal problem-solving language. They never spent time jockeying for power or spinning their wheels on the right approach; they just went after the problem together in the same fashion every time, solved it, and moved ahead. It was quite an amazing sight to see. Each of them knew their role and they did it well. That didn't mean they didn't disagree at times. In fact, Dave welcomed constructive arguments among the team. By the end of the argument, the team would always leave the space united, whether they were in complete agreement or not.

Scott and John were responsible for every part of a product's life cycle from the point a customer placed an order to the point we were paid for the order. They were accountable for every good and bad decision made by the team for those products they owned. Each of them also had a visual board to show their area's current state, future state, and the actions they were currently taking to move their team closer to the future state. These boards also included their goals and transformation metrics. Both Scott and John had specific goals for safety, quality, cost, delivery, and the morale of their team. These goals were posted and tracked on their visual boards.

Claudette, Ed, and Randy managed the day-to-day activities. You could say they were responsible for the tactical plans while Scott and John handled more strategic plans. Each supervisor had their own tactical plan that rolled up to either Scott or John's strategic plans. Scott and John's plans rolled up to Dave's site plans. Dave's site plans rolled up to the Division plans, and so on. A team member working at an assembly press could tell you how their work was directly related to Company Continuous Improvements overall company goals back at headquarters.

AVOIDING THE CONTINUOUS APPEARANCE TRAP

The supervisor team was also responsible for all escalation plans for the site. For example, every machine operator tracked their hourly output on a board. When they made their goal for the hour, they placed a green Solo cup above the board on a pin. When they missed their goal, they placed a red Solo cup. At any given moment, a supervisor could see at a glance how his or her area was performing. If a machine operator had three consecutive hours with a red cup, then they needed to notify a supervisor. Once the supervisor had a good understanding of the reason for missing their target, they would respond appropriately to the situation to ensure the machine did not continue to miss the target. When more than 25% of the machines in one area were red for an hour, then a red Solo cup was also placed on a peg near the site board. The escalation plan was very similar here. However, within an area, after three consecutive hours of misses, a task force was deployed to that area to include an engineer, maintenance manager, supervisor, and anyone else necessary to get the area turned around and back on track.

Rob worked on the production floor. He was a brilliant fabricator who could engineer and build anything you could imagine! His work was impeccable. We once carried out an improvement event on a machine where our goal was to reduce changeover times. These were automatic screw machines and after each run, they would be filled with metal shavings. The operators spent ten minutes spraying out the machines with a hose. The team came up with an idea to automate the spraying during the last ten minutes of the run and eliminate the spraying time while the machine was in changeover altogether. Dave gave Rob the freedom to be creative with clear boundaries around cost and resource usage. Rob designed and fabricated inexpensive sprayers inside the machines plumbed into the hose system and controlled by a valve he bought at the local hardware store. His experiment was a success! Dave asked Rob to build them for all the machines. However, once they were on all the machines, the team found that the water pressure was not strong enough to handle multiple machines at once. Ed devised a plan. He grabbed a drill and a handful of screws from

MEET THE TEAM

the maintenance crib and some alligator clips from the HR office, and asked Scott to laminate green and red cards. By lunch time, Ed had mounted the alligator clips on the top of each machine, visible to the entire crew, and created a system to stagger the changeovers with visual card signals. His idea worked great and changeovers were reduced by ten minutes apiece across all machines changing over multiple times a day...and it was a team effort!

Joining The Team

I must admit, when I first joined this team, I was a bit nervous. However, they invited me in and made me feel like we had been friends for years. They accepted me, even though I wasn't a local. They introduced me to their families, invited me into their homes, and always promoted family over work. They were caring, humble, and hard working.

As a member of the leadership team, I was responsible for certain products from order to cash—in other words, from the point a customer places an order to the point the customer paid for the product. I was also responsible for the metrics and even the financials. I was responsible for all the activities, machines, and people creating products for our global customers.

On my first day, Dave asked me to spend the next three weeks on the production floor running equipment. I remember thinking to myself, "This isn't what they hired me for." It wasn't until the three weeks were over that I understood the purpose. I was able to get to know the other team members in a way I never would have otherwise. I knew which ones were married and which had kids. I knew their kids' names and what sports they played. I knew what was important to some and not important to others.

Like Dave and his team, I was also immersed in Company Continuous Improvement's leadership and development programs which included learning about the Toyota Production System.

***

Continuous Improvement Defined

I made it pretty clear in my Introduction that Company Continuous Improvement is the example we all want to follow after reading this book. This is a good spot to explain in more detail why that is. Company Continuous Improvement taught me that continuous improvement is a total strategy that is applicable for any company, from any industry, and for any person, from anywhere in the world. While the practice of continuous improvement can be traced back before Toyota, its manufacturing origins were greatly inspired by the Toyota Production System, and the system has spread like a wildfire across the world since. As you learn about continuous improvement, you may also learn the term *lean*. The term *lean* was first introduced in 1990 in the book *The Machine That Changed The World*, where graduate student John Krafcik argued that lean means doing more with less. The concept of reducing or eliminating waste has also become an important part of continuous improvement because when waste is present, it causes a deviation from the perfect process. The perfect process gives the customer exactly what they want, when they want it, and in the amount they want, without interruption. Continuous improvement should be "the way we do things." I like to define continuous improvement as a worldwide attempt to develop a learning culture and implement this total strategy aimed at solving problems.

> **Continuous improvement should be 'the way we do things.' I like to define continuous improvement as a worldwide attempt to develop a learning culture and implement this total strategy aimed at solving problems.**

In May 1946, Shotaro Kamiya, the first president of Toyota Motor Sales

MEET THE TEAM

Co., Ltd. Japan, was the first Toyota executive to publicly declare that, "The primary focus must always be the customer." While this book gives you a framework by which you can assess your organization and leadership behaviors, it does not replace the teamwork, training, establishment of trust, having the right products, and the customer first promise enshrined in the Toyota Production System.

***

Now that we have covered the first company, let's learn about the second company.

Company Continuous *Appearance* was headquartered in a small city in the United States. Their factories can be found in other similar cities around the world. Company Continuous Appearance rarely promoted people into leadership roles from within the company. In fact, their entire executive leadership team was strategically recruited from surrounding manufacturers in an effort to bring in good talent from the outside. They had been around for a long time and many operators were nearing retirement. Their history goes all the way back to World War II. Many of the older workers take a lot of pride in their job and the company.

During my first tour of the factory, I noticed there seemed to be work-in-progress[*] product everywhere. Baskets of parts were lined up waiting to be moved to machines. Pallets of work-in-progress lined the aisleways and others were mixed in atop large mobile carts on casters.

I was introduced to a "team leader" in the area. I asked her about her team, and she explained that her role was not to oversee a team, but rather to make sure the team had the parts they needed to complete their work-in-progress. I asked her to explain further. She went on, "Every morning I receive a report of all the parts that were made last night. It's my job to find them and make sure they are queued up at the

---

[*] Work-in-progress, or in-process inventory are a company's partially finished goods waiting for completion. These items are either just being fabricated or waiting for further processing in a queue.

right process step. If I can't find them, then I talk to production control and they schedule another run of those parts. If they are hot, then I have to walk them through and make sure they get done on time."

We moved on to another department and as we walked, we began to discuss continuous improvement. My tour guide was very open and seemed to be very knowledgeable. When I asked if they had any experience with continuous improvement, he spouted, "We are already lean." (As a reminder: lean refers the process improvement methodology that, at its core, is focused on making value flow without interruptions and eliminating waste at every step through a business process.) I responded by asking him to *show me.*

For me, the key is in going to the shop floor or any place where value-creating work occurs. I love to observe the work being done, by those doing the work, at the place where the work is being done. This is the real work of the business: the value-creating work. Those working there must be involved in improvement activities if an organization is to ever establish a culture of continuous improvement.

The more I learned about Company Continuous Appearance, the more skeptical I became. I learned that many of the leaders had attended a few continuous improvement classes in the past, and some even had a certification or two. I was shown some great looking whiteboards with numbers and colors. I was told these were adopted based on something they had learned from an outside consultant or by watching a video. Once the boards were erected, they would call it done. For them, this meant the company had "arrived" and is now "lean."

The more time I spent with other leaders at Company Continuous Appearance, the more I learned about the various tools and techniques they were using. They would point to a shelf with some colored tape and order cards and say something like, "See this? We have a continuous improvement culture." But when I asked them what problem they were trying to solve or how many team members were involved, I would get blank stares or looks of total bewilderment.

MEET THE TEAM

They responded, "Why would we involve people with no experience in continuous improvement? We have experts that do this work."

Over time, I watched as the colored tape began to peel and fade, until eventually it was torn up and thrown in the trash. I began to find order cards collecting dust on shelves or under warehouse racks. Within time, the whiteboards and charts were not updated. I learned very quickly that true and sustainable change happens when those closest to the value-creating work are involved, empowered, and supported.

Chris

Chris was the plant manager and had come from a competitor company. He spent fifteen years working across town always in operations management. He was a smart man and a hard worker. He loved the idea of building a team and developing people. His kids were all grown up and out of the home. He and his wife were empty-nesters. Chris spent much of his free time on the golf course with his wife. They were both active with the local Rotary club and volunteered regularly with the homeless mission downtown.

Chris didn't spend a lot of time on production floor because he believed that was the job of his management team. There were two reasons you would find Chris out on the production floor. The first was whenever there was a significant problem such as a safety issue, missed shipment, or serious quality situation with an important customer. He would come out and everyone knew he was not happy; he walked very quickly and talked with his hands in the air. Chris did not accept any form of failure. The team never wanted to bring a problem to him. He always said, "Bring me solutions! I don't want to hear about your problems!"

The second reason you would find Chris on the production floor was during his once-a-month walk-about (which usually became his once-a-quarter walk-about). He would take a walk around the production floor to see how things were running and shake hands with people.

The problem was that because people rarely saw Chris, they weren't sure why he was out there. They weren't sure if he was there to yell or if he was evaluating their work. Either way, they changed their behavior knowing he could be watching. They seemed to become busier. They moved quicker. And they tried not to make eye contact.

Joining The Team

As part of the operations leadership team, I was responsible for a department with a group of machines and people within an order-to-cash product development process. There were other leaders responsible for other groups of machines, people, processes, and activities that made up the creation of one product for U.S. automobile makers. Once the unfinished product upstream from my department was ready, it was passed along to my team. After we added value to the product, then we passed it along to the next downstream process. We did not have any visibility into what was happening before our place in this workstream or after. I was responsible for the metrics in my department alone.

When I first joined the team, Chris asked me to be part of an ongoing book study. The operations team was studying a book by Jim Collins titled *Good to Great*. I still remember the first time I walked into the conference room. It was an early morning meeting and the room seemed dark. The light was not turned on, but sunlight was barely coming through the old vertical blinds hanging on the windows. Chris introduced me to the group.

The Team

Chris had one operations manager and four group leaders reporting to him and all were sitting at the table.

"Brian is my operations manager. He oversees all work on the production floor and is responsible for all decisions."

I would learn later that Brian was placed in this role as a stepping-

MEET THE TEAM

stone to bigger and better things. Chris was helping to develop Brian to become a plant manager at another factory and eventually, Brian would become an executive in the company. Brian was on the fast track to executive leadership after being identified as a high-potential leader in the company.

In meeting with Brian one day for lunch, I asked him what his biggest challenge in his role as operation manager was. His response was surprising. He told me that when he first took the role, he was excited to make real positive change. However, that excitement quickly went away when he was invited into Chris's office one day. Chris told him how much he appreciated the many improvement suggestions he was offering, but made it clear to him that this was not the place to create "unnecessary waves." Chris went on to tell him that the factory was performing well enough to not attract attention from upper management and he wanted to keep it that way. Brian was given direction to keep his head down, do what he is told, and soon enough, he would see the promotion to that plant manager role. Chris even gave him names of the two previous operations managers who had done just that and were now in executive positions in the company.

Chris continued his introductions, "Darrel and Todd are both first shift group leaders. Scott covers second shift and Tammy is our third shift group leader."

I looked at Scott and Tammy and with a chuckle, I said, "Wow, you two sure are dedicated to be here for an early morning book study."

It wasn't until a few weeks later when I found out they were mandated to attend all meetings with Chris on first shift. Sometimes they worked their normal shifts along with coming in on first shift, and other times they just stayed and worked the day shift, leaving their shift to be covered by their team leaders.

Overall, the company was doing well. The factory I would spend the next few years in was hitting its goals and everyone was happy...or were they?

Time spent with the team and a deeper look at the overall operations would soon reveal the truth about Company Continuous Appearance. The factory was unstable and in total chaos. The supervisors were in complete reaction mode. There were no escalation plans or hourly checks, just responding to the next "fire," hour after hour, day after day. The people were unhappy and coming to work to simply punch a clock. The leadership team spent their days trying to manage good people inside of a broken system.

And it didn't seem that anyone was ready to confront the brutal facts of our current reality, this culture of continuous appearance.

If only someone on the leadership team would have begun to ask the twelve questions you are about to read about in the following chapters. Maybe in your company, it will be you who asks the right questions!

QUESTION 1

Are You Content?

> "To be competitive, we have to look for every opportunity to improve efficiencies and productivity while increasing quality. Lean manufacturing principles have improved every aspect of our processes."
>
> ~Cynthia Fanning,
> Vice President at GE Appliances

The earliest form of a horse-drawn carriage was the chariot, which appeared in Mesopotamia around 3,000 BC. It was nothing more than a two-wheeled basin for a couple of people, pulled by one or two horses. Because it was light and quick, it was the favored vehicle for warfare with Egyptians. Over time, as carriages progressed, they eventually became the sole transportation method for the wealthy and elite.

Why don't we still use horse-drawn carriages as our preferred form of transportation? A horse-drawn carriage will get us from point A to point B; doesn't that fulfill the same function as an automobile? So why did we change?

People like Leonardo da Vinci, Simon Steven, Nicholas-Joseph Cugnot, Karl Benz, and Henry Ford were not content with the horse-drawn carriage. They believed there could be a faster and better way to get from point A to point B. In the 1500s, Leonardo da Vinci sketched a mechanized (horseless) cart. According to General Motors, in 1600,

QUESTION 1

a man named Simon Steven built a horseless chariot propelled by the wind, based on "sailing chariots" from China. Nicholas-Joseph Cugnot, a Frenchman, built a self-propelled vehicle with a steam engine in 1769. And finally, in 1886, Karl Benz patented the three-wheeled Motor Car, known as the "Motorwagen." It was the first true modern automobile. Benz eventually built a car company that still exists today as the Daimler Group. While Henry Ford did not invent the automobile, he developed and manufactured the first automobile that middle-class Americans could afford. Ford changed the way of life for many people with his vision to make owning a car both practical and affordable.

Every day, new ideas are generated all over the world. New products are created and developed. Existing products are improved. New methods are executed. So many people are looking at problems in different ways and coming up with new and innovative solutions, offering a never-ending stream of value to the companies they work for.

Imagine if Ford had released the Model T and then simply stopped: no innovation, no consideration of competition, no improvements. Would Ford Motor Company exist today? What if Karl Benz would have stopped with the Motorwagen as it was originally developed?

Is your organization content with your current operations? Or are you seeking out greater opportunities to develop new and/or improved products and processes for your customers?

For some organizations, creating dissatisfaction with the current state is easy. Maybe your business is not performing well, and you are losing sales. Or maybe you are not fulfilling your mission. In these cases, it would be easy to communicate and create alignment around why you need to change. However, the situation is not always this clear-cut.

Let's imagine now that your current output is top-notch. Is that enough for you to stop innovating and stop reaching for more? Other companies are racing to catch up and pass you. Standing still, in effect, is the same as moving backwards.

Organizations should be focused on turning ideas into new and/or improved processes to create, improve, or expand business capabilities. The goal is to create an organization that learns, improves, and innovates permanently. As we develop this constant dissatisfaction with the status quo, we create an enormous organizational capability to generate new ideas and solutions all the time.

> **The goal is to create an organization that learns, improves, and innovates permanently.**

Develop Dissatisfaction With The Status Quo

Employees should love their work but feel uncomfortable, or dissatisfied, when they feel things are staying the same, or not improving. There should be an urgency to improve and create more value for the customer. Many times I am asked how to create this dissatisfaction with the status quo. How do we compel people to get involved in a change initiative? Or, can we create an environment where people willingly have dissatisfaction with the status quo?

I want to be careful here not to suggest that leaders should focus only on dissatisfaction, as this can drive teams to burn out. Every improvement, or learning from an improvement experiment, should be followed up with a celebration of success. Celebrations don't have to be a big, orchestrated event. Rather, sometimes they can be as

> **While we do want to create a sense of urgency toward change and improvement, we don't want to create an unnecessary panic.**

QUESTION 1

simple as recognizing effort and success at a daily stand-up meeting.

While we do want to create a sense of urgency toward change and improvement, we don't want to create an unnecessary panic. I have heard many leaders use the term "burning platform" to create panic with the goal of coercing people away from the status quo. For some companies, they may be experiencing a real emergency situation. For those leaders, I recommend complete transparency. Increased communication around the emergency and what team members can do to help is always the right approach. However, conjuring up a burning platform when there isn't one is just plain wrong.

Do you have a compelling story? A compelling story is a narrative that charts a change over time, demonstrating how potential solutions fit into certain problems you are experiencing. This story can generate more engagement from listeners than any burning platform ever will. Your team needs to trust the importance of a pragmatic, accurate, and open portrayal of the initiative. Are your competitors improving? If so, then you can create a compelling story specific to your competition. Can you serve more people with improvements on the current state? Try telling that story!

> **A compelling story is a narrative that charts a change over time, demonstrating how potential solutions fit into certain problems you are experiencing**

By telling a compelling story, you can clarify your team's motivation to develop discontent with the status quo. Let the story show them where you've come from and where you might go. The story must be consistent and adopted by all leaders in the organization. The leadership team should weave in the compelling story at all opportunities. They should ask their teams constantly, "What's next?" "How can we make that even better?" "How did you improve your work area today?"

Constantly communicating dissatisfaction with the status quo will drive team members to action. As you look forward in time, no process can, or even should, stay the same for long. Those who are closest to the value-creating work will have new ideas. Those ideas should be used to challenge the current way of doing things and reset it to a new level.

One area to experiment with in developing dissatisfaction with the status quo is not only to tell the story, but to create constant reminders for your teams about their external competitors. Most humans are competitive by nature, and when they know their competitors are improving, they will want to follow suit. In competitive markets, companies must continue to improve and evolve or they will cease to exist. To maintain market share, companies must improve with the market. If they want to gain market share, they must improve and innovate even faster. The market always wants more.

I once accompanied a group on a tour of their competitor's experience center, which was open to the public. The competitor was double the size of this particular company and owned a large part of the market share. The leaders from the company were not looking to steal any ideas; rather, they wanted their team to see what could happen if they continued to work hard and improve operations. They celebrated their competitor's success while also creating a healthy dissatisfaction with their current state. The team members came back excited to make improvements!

What if you are working with a service organization and don't have competitors? In that case, you might connect the compelling story to your mission and purpose. For example, at Remembrance Ranch, a non-profit organization I founded in 2005, we are always looking for opportunities to improve. Our staff meets after each summer camp and answers the following questions: What went well? What didn't go well? What can we do and how can we serve families better? Every

QUESTION 1

year, we make improvements to our program and create opportunities for cost reductions. If we are able to improve and reduce costs, then we can serve more families with our mission to transform lives. People will support change when they see and experience a purposeful connection to an organizational mission.

Another area to experiment with is to communicate customer expectations to the entire team on a regular basis. Customer expectations could include production standards, quality standards, delivery standards, or mission standards. The most important consideration is your customer. Without customers, you would not be in business. Yet customer needs are continually changing. You may have exactly what your customer needs today, but tomorrow they may need something else. To stay current with your customers' needs, you need to be innovative. Seek out improvements in the development stage of new products and processes. You cannot meet the needs of customers long-term unless you recognize the importance of innovation and act on it. If you fail to innovate, your business will fail to grow.

In his book *Designing The Future**, Dr. Jeffrey Liker says, "There seems to be a natural attraction to improvement activities that focus on current operations, mostly in manufacturing and labor reductions. Quite frankly, we are a bit confused by this. Certainly, reducing operating costs and improving how products and services are delivered is of great value. However, there are far greater opportunities to do this in the development stage of products and processes. Successful new products can increase revenue, margin, and market share and create a halo effect that can change the way your organization is perceived."

Finally, make your improvement approach simple and visual. Your team doesn't need complex algorithms to know they need to improve. Consider the best way to present real, accurate, and updated data and/or metrics in a way that everyone can understand. Metric charts coupled with leadership commitment can communicate what is

---
* Jeffrey K. Liker and James M. Morgan, Designing The Future (US: McGraw-Hill, 2019)

important and necessary to change. In his book, *Measures of Success*[*], Mark Graban says, "A chart will always tell us more than a list of numbers."

In the traditional world of management, you may be familiar with red, yellow, and green metric charts. Red is bad, green is good, and yellow is somewhere between. This can be used to tell a compelling story; however, you must be careful! In an environment where people are scared to fail, some pressured managers may lobby heavily for easily achievable goals so they don't have to explain why they have "failed." However, this is the wrong mindset! Red does not mean you have failed; rather, it means there is an opportunity. Leaders should be excited to know where the problems are so they can go after the problems, and not blame their people. They must never view problems as a distraction, but rather as an inciting force for continuous improvement and new opportunities. "Green" boards are worthless if left green too long. Celebrate the green, then reset your goals. If you are green too long, your team won't know where to focus improvement efforts.

One of my favorite stories about creating dissatisfaction with the status quo using internal competition comes from the early 1900s when steel magnate Charles M. Schwab used a piece of chalk and the number 6 to create some healthy internal competition. According to Carnegie's book *How to Win Friends & Influence People*[**], the story went like this:

> *"This conversation took place at the end of the day just before the night shift came on. Schwab asked the manager for a piece of chalk, then, turning to the nearest man, asked:*
>
> *'How many heats did your shift make today?'*
>
> *'Six'*
>
> *Without another word, Schwab chalked a big figure 6 on the floor, and walked away. When the night shift came in, they*

---

[*] Mark Graban, Measures of Success (US: Constancy Inc., 2019)
[**] Carnegie, Dale, How To Win Friends and Influence People (New York: Simon & Schuster, 2009)

QUESTION 1

saw the 6 and asked what it meant. 'The big boss was in here today the day people said.' He asked us how many heats we made, and we told him six. He chalked it down on the floor.

The next morning Schwab walked through the mill again. The night shift had rubbed out 6 and replaced it with a big seven.

When the day shift reported for work the next morning, they saw a big 7 chalked on the floor. So the night shift thought they were better than the day shift did they? Well, they would show the night shift a thing or two. The crew pitched in with enthusiasm, and when they quit that night, they left behind them an enormous, swaggering 10. Things were stepping up.

Shortly this mill, which had been lagging way behind in production, was turning out more work than any other mill in the plant."

Schwab's strategy instantly created a rivalry between the day and night shift crew because it's natural to try to enhance the status of your own team.

"The way to get things done is to stimulate competition," Schwab told Carnegie.

Case Study: Company Continuous Improvement Vs. Company Continuous Appearance

Company Continuous Appearance was doing billions of dollars in sales annually. Unfortunately, because the company was doing so well, they had minimal discussions around expenses. Managers were not responsible for profit and loss. In fact, most team members did not hear about the financial status of the company or their factories outside of the few company-wide meetings where they were given very high-level summaries. Teams were content with the status quo, and wasteful practices became acceptable because they were making so much money. Most factories didn't even track their scrap or defect rates.

During this time, Brian introduced me to a temporary employee working on a production line. He was checking 100% of the parts on the line for a printed barcode. If the barcode was not there, he was to place the part in a rework tote. The company leader told me they had had a customer complaint the previous year and this was their response to assure the customer did not get another part without a barcode. I moved further up the production line to the bar coder machine and found a broken vision system, which had been installed to automatically check for barcodes, in place just after the bar coder machine. I asked Brian about the vision system. His response was, "It was easier for us to put a person on the line to check than to fix the vision system."

I asked, "Do you know how much that person is costing you in comparison to fixing the vision system?"

He responded, "Why should we care? We make enough money to not worry about these things."

Should he have cared? Absolutely! The team at Company Continuous Appearance had become satisfied in the status quo. Financially, they were doing great. This level of comfort allowed them to accept wasteful actions which greatly impacted the bottom line.

It was a completely opposite picture at Company Continuous Improvement. There wasn't a day that went by there when Dave and the rest of the leadership team weren't communicating a compelling story for improvement. Whether they were reviewing competitor headlines, communicating alignment with future goals, or promoting active problem-solving to improve KPIs, the team was receiving a clear and consistent message: Never accept the status quo!

As I mentioned earlier, creating healthy competition internally can also spark dissatisfaction with the status quo. Company Continuous Appearance didn't care much about competition because they felt

QUESTION 1

comfortable in their current state. In contrast, Company Continuous Improvement scheduled best-practice sharing tours. Teams were scheduled to go see other teams' areas and benchmark for success. The team presenting would provide a tour map with specific stops to bring outside teams through their area. At each stop, a team member would present a best practice. They would provide some background and "before" metrics followed up with the improved future state and "after" metrics. At the end of the tour, Claudette, Randy or Ed would present total monthly or quarterly savings due to their improvements. Dave used these best practice tours to create some healthy competition between the teams, and even created a trophy for the winning team to place in their area until another team could win it away from them.

Teams at Company Continuous Improvement also conducted cleanliness audits of each other's areas with very clear guidelines. All audit results were posted and each month, the team with the lowest cleanliness score would receive the golden toilet seat award. This was Rob's idea and he created the trophy after a quick trip to the plumbing department at the local hardware store. The golden toilet seat award recipients received a gold-painted toilet seat to hang above their area until the next round of audits. As I am sure you can imagine, teams did not enjoy having the golden toilet seat hanging in their area. They worked very hard to meet cleanliness guidelines laid out in the audit to assure the toilet seat didn't stay in their area another month! All audit results were charted, and teams could see with a glance where they were in relationship to the other areas. This created some fun, healthy competition to keep the teams motivated and excited about continuous improvement.

Your Call To Action

Are you content? If you are content, then your team will also be content.

A dissatisfaction for the status quo cannot be instilled by pushing urgency; you must plan and organize steps built around leadership and empowering people.

First, consider a challenge to develop and get the right transformational leadership in the right place. The following chapters will help you determine whether you have the right leaders in the right positions, and what development is necessary to support change in your organization.

Next, ensure that your people understand their contribution to the overall strategy. Don't just assume they know. When you meet them at the place where the value-creating work is being done, ask them directly. Make things fun by brainstorming and experimenting with forms of totems in your work areas that create healthy internal competition and stand as reminders of external competition.

Eliminate the need for complex algorithms communicating the need for change. Through experimentation, determine how to best define success, and begin measuring it visually.

Explore target conditions that will create dissatisfaction with the status quo. Through experimentation and by engaging your team, learn how you can best communicate dissatisfaction with the current state while maintaining your employees' excitement in their daily work.

Focus your experimentation on turning ideas into new and/or improved processes to create, improve, or expand business capabilities. The goal is to create teams that learn, improve, and innovate permanently.

If you don't already have a simple process for introducing new products and processes into your organization, then now is the time to begin. Involve your team in the process allowing involvement at all levels. By doing this, the engagement will create ownership and excitement in the future of the organization.

QUESTION 1

Answer all questions using the following abbreviations:

1=No 2=Sometimes 3=Mostly 4=Yes/Always

ARE YOU CONTENT?	
1. Do you communicate a compelling story and vision for growth?	
2. Are you putting out new and innovative products or services?	
3. Are teams discussing improvements?	
4. Are methods and processes being improved?	
5. Is someone assessing the competition and suggesting improvements?	
QUESTION 1 TOTAL	

Transfer your total to the full assessment at the end of the book. Compare totals to establish a priority.

QUESTION 2

Where Are Your Leaders Spending Their Time?

> "Show me your calendar and I'll tell you your priorities."
>
> ~Quint Studer, Author and Founder of the Studer Community Institute

One of the first things I ask my coaching clients is to send me a screenshot of their calendar. This may seem weird, but it helps us start a conversation about their priorities. For example, many of us say we put family first, but how many of us actually block time in our calendars for family? Or maybe you say your health is important. If we open your calendar, will we see that you block time to work out? To get our priorities straight, we have to begin by taking stock of where we spend our time. We may need to change where we are spending time if we want a different result. It's the same for our continuous improvement initiatives.

To sustain the continuous improvement initiatives we build, we also will need to institute a different leadership system and a different management system. If we don't, the whole process will fall apart. If we manage the same way, with the same meetings and same metrics, we will get the same behaviors, beliefs, and the same results. Therefore, unless we change the way we manage, we will fail at sustaining our continuous improvement initiatives. How do you manage differently?

QUESTION 2

Start by taking an assessment of where your leaders spend their time.

One of the greatest barriers to establishing a culture of continuous improvement is that leaders avoid spending time in the place where the value-creating work is being done. That location should be the starting point for any continuous improvement journey. No one knows better about what is happening with the product or service better than those who are closest to the work.

If the value-creating work is outside a computer, office, or meeting room, then leaders cannot expect different results if they are sitting in a corner office and only attending KPI meetings. If your front-line and mid-management leaders are not spending most of their time where the value-creating work is being done, then the behavior of your leaders must change.

> **One of the greatest barriers to establishing a culture of continuous improvement is that leaders avoid spending time in the place where the value-creating work is being done.**

Leaders should also be committed to self-development and have the support to do so. Later in this book, I will offer some specific actions to help leaders understand what self-development really looks like. While they are developing themselves as leaders, they should use their newly-acquired knowledge to coach others simultaneously. To facilitate the structure of coaching, I always suggest a 1:5 ratio of team leader to team members, with a massive commitment to developing leaders.

Many organizations have little in the way of documented best practices for where and how leaders are spending their time. Supervisors, managers, and directors are left with only their job description to guide their daily activities. Given this reality, it's not surprising that many people fail to start, cultivate, spread, and sustain the continuous improvement mindset. Ask yourself what systems you have in place to document how and where your leaders are spending their time, and it may become easier to guide them to invest where value is being created.

Leader Standard Work

The performance of your leaders is directly correlated to where they are spending their time and when. Leader standard work is a tool that can help leaders spend their time in the right place and at the right time. Think of leader standard work as a necessary list of activities to sustain the lean management system. It includes a set of actions, tools, and behaviors that we block time for and incorporate into the daily activities of leaders at all levels. Leader standard work must be documented, practiced consistently, and changed only with reflection and experimentation. Because leader standard work is visual and is specific in the sequence and time of day in which tasks are performed, it is useful for driving actions and learning.

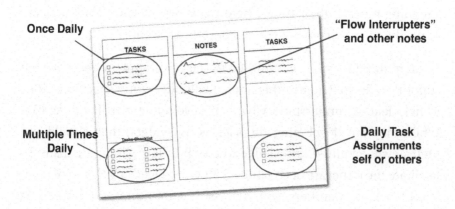

The basic output of leader standard work is a list of daily activities for leaders to follow. The list includes important actions to be completed daily; some only need to be done once per day, while others may need to be performed multiple times a day. Examples might include stand-up meetings, visual board reviews, audits, and coaching.

Unless all leaders in your organization have, and follow, leader standard work, then your leadership and team won't perceive much value in leader standard work. Demonstrating a commitment to leader standard work sets a precedent for standardization when it comes time to develop process standards, and shows that no one in your organization is above this tool. Let's think about some professions that put a high priority on standard work. Airline pilots, surgeons, and astronauts all have a variety of checklists and predictable procedures they must follow. Would you want to board a flight if you knew the crew skipped all their checklists? What about medical doctors or astronauts? They use leader standard work. Do your leaders think their work is above open-heart surgery and rocket science?

Who should use leader standard work? Everyone.

ROLE	% of Work (time that should be standardized	
Executives	10-15%	Standard work is LESS structured • % of time standard • Specific sequence • Specific time of day • More time for discretionary tasks
Support Department Managers	25%	
Value Stream Managers	50%	
Value Stream Support Staff	80%	Standard work is MORE structured • % of time standard • Specific sequence • Specific time of day • Less time for discretionary tasks
Team Leaders	80%	
Operators (Associates)	95% +	

Leader standard work benefits the entire organization. As you can see in the figure above, the percentage of work time devoted to leader standard work will vary depending on your role in the organization.

Deploying leader standard work at all levels and roles in an organization will result in behavior and thinking modification, which is necessary for culture change. As you begin to use leader standard work in your team interactions, people will start to see your questions in a positive light. They will start to anticipate your checklist as a necessary part of the day, instead of assuming something is wrong. This shift in thinking creates teachable moments that no leader should ignore. Opportunities to improve will surface much sooner, and as an organization you'll be able to learn together what is working and what isn't. Creating a culture that learns together creates a culture that can sustain improvements together.

> **Deploying leader standard work at all levels and roles in an organization will result in behavior and thinking modification, which is necessary for culture change.**

***

In most work environments, every day is different. Things happen, and plans must change, sometimes by the hour. Leaders need to be flexible and able to adapt to respond properly in less predictive environments. Does that mean when the day doesn't go as planned you just throw out your leader standard work and plan to pick it back up tomorrow?

No.

No matter what happens each day, at a minimum the daily standard work list must be accomplished. There may be different activities that happen on different days of the week, at different times, or on different shifts, but these must be accomplished as part of the lean management system. They are non-negotiable because they are the actions and behaviors that support the culture you are trying to create. They will result in the output you are striving for. They will bring you closer to your long-term goals.

It's important that a leader's standard work is timely. A predictable, scheduled spot check of metrics can prevent an abnormality from becoming a crisis. Recurring operational checks can raise a red flag if important metrics are suffering. Note: Leaders must be careful not to overreact to noise. Perhaps there are roadblocks, or barriers, that are preventing team members from achieving their goal. Only when a leader is aware of these obstacles can they begin to remove them. These hurdles can be identified and addressed immediately or moved to a scheduled improvement event for further analysis and resolution. When a scheduled task, such as a spot check of metrics, is left up to the discretion of the individual, it can be overlooked.

Leader standard work can be a powerful tool to help leaders shift behavior to focus on the process rather than the person. Leader standard work is process dependent, not person dependent. How many times have you heard, "They just aren't doing it right," or "It's hard to find good help these days?" It's much easier to blame people: the people who do the work, the people who designed the process, or the people who lead the team. If you can remember, "It's always the process, not the person," you are on your way to building the trust you need to solve your problems. Leader standard work also provides continuity of operations (when leaders are on vacation, new, etc.) and raises the bar for leadership staff.

With clearly documented standards, a leader's expectations are clear. There is no room for doubt. Either the current best practice is getting followed, or it's not. These clear expectations remove the feelings often associated with someone's work performance. Often, we hear someone say, "I don't *think* he is doing a good job", or "I don't *think* she is doing it right". With leader standard work, it is either getting done, or it isn't.

These predictable tasks also are used as a baseline for future system improvements. If the leader standard work duties are not adding value, we can evaluate them and adjust accordingly. Simply put, leader standard work eliminates the guesswork and discretionary activities that are often non-value added.

How to Deploy Leader Standard Work

The process for establishing leader standard work is as important as the work itself. You will need to lay out a method for designing and managing the process. This is a great time to involve the team that works in the area. Ask the team to describe the process and highlight the critical activities. Who is responsible for the critical activities? Ask the other team members what information is lacking for them to make informed, everyday decisions. You can use this insight to add data the team would find valuable for collection and reporting in your leader standard work.

You also need to determine the frequency of each task you add to your leader standard work. Some actions will be daily, and some hourly. Remember those red flags indicating when metrics are suffering? This data is not something we want to learn about at the end of the shift when it's too late to address the issue. Hourly checks help us to make corrections or adjustments before a problem gets out of hand. Be sure to consider other shifts that run in the area. Make sure everyone knows no matter what happens each day, at a minimum, the daily standard work list must be accomplished, and the leader responsible is aware of their responsibility.

> **Do not let perfection get in the way of progress.**

Start with something and try it. Do not let perfection get in the way of progress. Leader standard work is a living document, meaning it

QUESTION 2

needs to change as our need for valuable data and improved processes change. The data we collect today might not be the data we collect tomorrow. That's okay. Recording what works and what doesn't is the way we use this tool as a baseline for improvement. If you find yourself modifying your leader standard work, congratulations. You are doing it right.

Leaders should carry the checklist with them and update the posted data continuously. Updating data regularly prevents someone from going back and filling out the records at the end of the shift. However, people should not be criticized for not filling out their sheets. A blank sheet is a symptom of a problem and should prompt a problem-solving discussion. Why is the checklist blank? Why didn't you have time? What is keeping you from filling it out? Is there an obstacle preventing you that needs to be removed?

Standard work is always our best-known method for completing a task. Following the Plan-Do-Check/Study-Act (PDCA) cycle is the way we can improve on our best-known methods. Think of it this way, the PLAN is the actual standard work we are following. Then we DO the task and record the data. This gives us a chance to discuss, study and/or CHECK, what is working or not, and if we learned anything from the data. We then ACT, or adjust the standard, based on what we learned from observing the CHECK step. This cycle is what makes leader standard work so powerful. Over time our standards will evolve, and instead of feeling like extra work, the standard work will be useful and effective.

It's important to teach the how and why of leader standard work instead of just adding another management tool to the tool box. This approach allows us to coach leaders while they develop their own system. It's important that we encourage them to have a system that evolves over time to better suit their team's needs. After all, if we are creating something that does not currently exist, it only makes sense to involve the people who will be using it.

I have been asked many times if executives should also be following leader standard work. As I mentioned earlier, the answer is yes. Every leader in an organization should be using leader standard work. However, we must acknowledge that the higher a person goes in the organization the harder it is to standardize what they do. That's okay. Many companies have LPAs, or Layered Process Audits, that executives participate in. These LPAs are a leader's standard work. Leave open time blocks and flexibility in the schedule if you are including managers and executives in your deployment. Earlier I mentioned that executives might have 10-15 percent of their day standardized. Managers typically fall in the 30 percent range, while team leaders and supervisors have the highest percentage of their time standardized with leader standard work.

Lean success is sustained when leaders and managers help develop an environment and structure that is conducive to learning and sharing ideas. Empower your workforce to try new things and let the data be their guide to the next steps that produce process improvements at their level of the work. Let them improve the process at the level that they truly own. Breaking down barriers, and fostering continuous improvement is the responsibility of the leader. Encourage PDCA. Give the team the data they ask for. Take regular Gemba* walks and show them you take your leader standard work seriously. Involve them in the decision process. Sustaining the gains is easier when the team realizes improvements on their own. After all, we are creating future leaders.

Case Study: Company Continuous Improvement Vs. Company Continuous Appearance

When Brian was promoted at Company Continuous Appearance, I was given responsibility for the three-shift operation reporting directly to Chris, the plant manager. I was excited about the opportunity to make real change in this operation. Within my first few weeks as the

---

* Gemba (Genba) is a Japanese term meaning "the real place." The Gemba Walk is an opportunity for staff to stand back from their day-to-day tasks to walk the floor of their workplace to identify wasteful activities.

operations manager, I was able to confirm a terrifying reality: there seemed to be an "us versus them" mentality between those team members doing the value-creating work and the leadership team. There were remnants of continuous improvement work, but most of it was very surface-level. There was a list of action items on one wall with no owners and a few due dates; very little was complete and most due dates were already past. Some action items were over four months old. The only way I would be able to really understand what was truly going on was to meet with each person individually and ask them. So that's exactly what I did. I met with each of the team members and leaders, one on one, and completed an Empowerment Continuum. (You will learn about this later.) I asked each of them the same three questions:

1. What is going WELL in this operation?

2. What is NOT going WELL in this operation?

3. Do you have any ideas for how we can improve the operation?

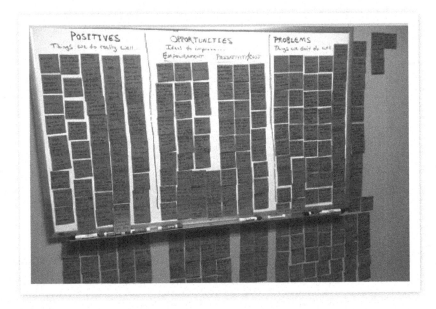

Why do you think I asked each person the exact three questions? By asking each person the exact three questions, the resulting data could be analyzed for patterns.

Because I am a visual person, I placed the answers to these questions on a wall behind me using Post-it notes of different colors. Positives represent those things that are going well. Problems are the headaches and those things not going well. Opportunities are different from Problems because they offer a potential solution or initiative that will assist the team to reach a goal.

The results were amazing!

Upon completion of this exercise, I had learned a lot about the operation and the people doing the value-creating work. My next step was to cluster the Post-it notes and find out if there were any consistent themes or patterns. Here is a picture of the "Problems/Opportunities" section.

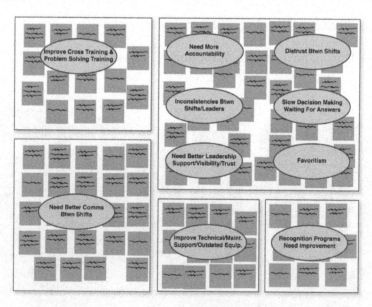

When I summarized the results of this exercise, one constant theme began to emerge: Our management system was broken and leader behavior was a contributor. The team didn't feel like they were being listened to or respected. When they brought up an idea for improvement, management would shoot it down or implement something completely different. The team said management had no idea what was really going on in the operation because they were never out on the shop floor. These comments were really disturbing. I was ready to present my report to the plant manager.

Chris was not surprised by my findings. He admitted that he had withdrawn from the shop floor over the past few years. He was being asked to manage larger initiatives outside the plant and was placing most of the plant responsibilities on his group leaders. Because he was outside the plant more than he was inside, Chris did most of his managing through email and expected his group leaders to respond almost immediately when he gave direction. He also invited all the supervisors (including 2nd and 3rd shift) to attend all meetings for the plant, most of which took place between the hours of 8 am and 3 pm. This was pulling all group leaders off the shop floor and into meetings or behind their computer screen. They were stretched to the limit and not able to respond to the requests of their team members. Chris was trying to use the operations manager position to help with the situation. He hoped this would solve all their problems. The management team, including the plant manager, needed a complete overhaul, starting with a new management system.

***

Leadership structure and expectations were different at Company Continuous Improvement. Here, every leader was trained and expected to follow leader standard work. This was not optional. It was the expected way to manage. The company trained leaders in all aspects of their leader standard work: waste and Gemba walks, visual boards, layered audits, coaching, problem solving, and so on.

Every leader understood how their leader's standard work was connected to the company's long-term vision. The company vision gave them something to rally around and their leader standard work established those actionable steps and behaviors that helped make the connection.

Dave blocked time for a daily Gemba walk with Scott, John and me. We had a shared calendar visually posted for the entire factory team with all stand-up meetings that we all had to attend, while the other tier meetings were the responsibility of the supervisors. Ed, Randy, and Claudette held daily stand-up meetings with their team at the same time and place every day. The supervisor desk was located in the center of the production floor; however, you would hardly ever find them there after the morning meeting. After their stand-up meetings, their days were completely planned out with hourly Gemba walks to review their teams' hour-by-hour boards, audit, and coach. And problems that arose would be dealt with immediately. Any issues in need of further problem solving or in need of being escalated were the responsibility of the supervisor. Every Friday, Scott, John, and I would meet with the supervisors to discuss any problems that caused a deviation from the standard. For any recurring problems, we would discuss whether we needed to begin a root cause analysis or if we needed to collect more data to ensure we could properly define the problem. Either way, action was taken.

At Company Continuous Improvement, some daily items found on a supervisor's leader standard work would include lead/attend tier meetings, audit standard work, Gemba walk, metric/team board checks, coaching time, and safety audits.

Your Call To Action

Where are your leaders spending the majority of their time today? Is that where you want them to spend their time? If not, then create a challenge for your leadership team to change where they spend the majority of their time.

If you want different results, you need to change your management system. Leader standard work is a powerful tool to help leaders shift behavior to focus on the process. Leader standard work is process-dependent, not person-dependent. Every leader in your organization should have some form of leader standard work.

QUESTION 2

To drive leader accountability, your organizational leader standard work should include clearly documented expectations, and should be made visual to everyone. By keeping leader standard work posted and visual, all team members can see if process, quality, or employee concerns are being addressed, and if opportunities for improvement are getting a leader's attention. Leader standard work is a living document, meaning it needs to change as a leader learns more and as processes improve. The data we collect today might not be the data we collect tomorrow. That's okay. Recording what works and what doesn't is the way we use this tool as a baseline for improvement.

Answer all questions using the following abbreviations:

1=No 2=Sometimes 3=Mostly 4=Yes/Always

HOW ARE YOUR LEADERS SPENDING THEIR TIME?	
1. Do team and mid-level leaders spend the majority of their time where the value-add work is being done?	
2. Do executive leaders spend some time where the value-add work is being done?	
3. Do leaders have some type of leader standard work?	
4. Is the right percentage of each leaders work standardized?	
5. Do leaders discuss and make improvements to time-management?	
QUESTION 2 TOTAL	

Transfer your total to the full assessment at the end of the book. Compare totals to establish a priority.

QUESTION 3

Are You Pursuing Perfection?

> "Perfection is not attainable. But if we chase perfection, we can catch excellence."
>
> ~Vince Lombardi, NFL Head Coach

Every organization exists for a purpose. The organization's purpose should engage its people and drive all daily activity. A vision gives a clear, specific picture of what the organization would look like if it met or achieved this purpose at some time in the future.

Toyota's long-term vision is to achieve zero defects, 100% value added work, one-piece flow, and security for their people. They exist for this purpose. This vision is ideal and is probably impossible to achieve; however, it provides direction for the organization. But creating a commitment to pursue a vision of perfection can be challenging. If the vision isn't fully possible, how do we get the team excited about it?

In 1519, Hernán Cortés arrived in the New World with six hundred men and made history by destroying his ships. He believed that his group's purpose was to conquer the New World. By destroying his ships, he communicated a commitment to this vision and sent a clear message to his men: There is no turning back. Two years later, he succeeded in his conquest of the Aztec empire.

While I am not suggesting you burn any ships, I am challenging you to determine your vision and generate a complete commitment to pursue this perfect vision. Henry Ford didn't burn any ships, but he did generate a commitment to his vision.

What can we learn from Cortés and Ford? Even if reaching full realization of a vision isn't possible, creating a total commitment to that vision is surely possible. First, the organization must create the vision. Second, the organization needs to establish clear and consistent communication of that vision. Finally, the organization should define and establish accountability around how its people should behave. Once support of the vision and values has been established, the team will have a guideline for decision making and organizational direction.

> **Even if reaching full realization of a vision isn't possible, creating a total commitment to that vision is surely possible.**

True North: Identify Your "Perfection"

The 20-mile North Country Trail and Manistee River Trail loop in northern Michigan is my favorite backpacking trail. The first time I took my daughter with me, I printed a map of the trail and packed it in my backpack. I had hiked the trail myself many times, but in case she got disoriented, I wanted to be sure my daughter knew where we were going. When we arrived, my daughter gazed out at the many trails forking off from the trailhead and asked, "Where do we go from here?"

I pulled out the map I had printed off and said with a smile, "It depends on where we want to get to."

She replied, "Dad, I don't care where we go."

AVOIDING THE CONTINUOUS APPEARANCE TRAP

I couldn't help but think about the scene in Alice In Wonderland[*] when Alice meets Cheshire Puss:

> *'Cheshire Puss,' she began, rather timidly, as she did not at all know whether it would like the name: however, it only grinned a little wider. 'Come, it's pleased so far,' thought Alice, and she went on. 'Would you tell me, please, which way I ought to go from here?'*
>
> *'That depends a good deal on where you want to get to,' said the Cat.*
>
> *'I don't much care where—' said Alice.*
>
> *'Then it doesn't matter which way you go,' said the Cat.*
>
> *'—so long as I get somewhere,' Alice added as an explanation.*
>
> *'Oh, you're sure to do that,' said the Cat, 'if you only walk long enough.'*

While standing at the trailhead with our backpacks lying next to us, I explained the importance of charting our course prior to setting out. If we do not set our course before we begin, I said, we will be walking with no end in mind. How will we ever know when we have arrived? If we do not know where we are going, we may miss things along the way that are important. How will we know if we are getting closer to our True North?

True North is a key concept in continuous improvement. Continuous

> **We know that opportunities for improvement will never end, but that doesn't mean we can, or should, work on all of them as they present themselves.**

---
[*] Lewis Carroll, Alice's Adventures in Wonderland (New York: Macmillan, 1920)

improvement is a journey: There is no absolute destination point, and we will never achieve perfection. So think of True North not as a destination, but as a term used to describe the ideal state of perfection that your organization should be continually striving for.

This continual striving is an important part of keeping your eye on your North Star. We know that opportunities for improvement will never end, but that doesn't mean we can, or should, work on all of them as they present themselves. My daughter and I could have bounced around from trail to trail, walking here and there, and would never have really made it anywhere. Only when all team members engage in a persistent practice toward True North can organizations become first class.

When I finally placed the map in front of my daughter, we surveyed the different options along the trails: a waterfall, an amazing overlook, and a suspension bridge. She pointed at the suspension bridge and said, "I want to go here."

If we didn't choose our True North and chart our course prior to leaving, we may have never made it to the suspension bridge…or we may have been lost in the forest or walking in circles for days!

What's your True North?

Communicating Your Vision

To reach organizational alignment on your vision, you'll need to create a concise communication strategy aimed at all stakeholders. First, make your vision visible to your entire organization. You have made the commitment and taken the time to determine perfection and direction for your organization, so don't let it become a statement that sits on a memo in a desk drawer. Rather, post it where everyone can see it daily and include it in all key messages. Be sure to include your vision in all internal and external communications.

Get creative in how your vision is communicated. Develop your vision GPS, but don't just hand out maps and hope they make it. Travel alongside your team, stay out in front, and give direction. Create a story around your vision that can be told by anyone in your organization.

Second, ensure that the message is consistent and agreed upon by all leaders. Take measures to ensure that the leadership team speaks with one voice about your vision and values. Create metaphors, figures of speech, and slogans around your vision. If you show excitement and pride, then your leadership team will also be proud to communicate your organizational vision.

Third, engage your entire team. Make every effort to seek the opinions and ideas of your people to help drive the vision forward. Consistently show how the vision is contributing to work throughout the entire organization and how each person is contributing to the vision. Bolster what you are saying with your behavior. Choose a few true engagement stories you can repeat regularly to demonstrate commitment to vision and values.

Finally, communicate your vision and values through as many channels as possible. Establish a formal marketing campaign to utilize internal newsletters, website, social media, and onboarding to put out a consistent message promoting alignment to the vision.

QUESTION 3

Communicating vision will only get you so far; the next step is to align the behaviors of your organization with the vision.

How Should People Behave?

People want to know what good looks like: how they can define success for their work day. Organizations that align their core values with success measures communicate a simple message about behavior to their people: If X is important and it's measured by Y, how do we need to behave to achieve success? By developing challenge questions for your team, you can help them receive a clear message regarding behavior.

Business Values Assessment Grid				
	Challenge Questions			
Toyota Values / **KPIs - Ideal State**	**Customer First**	**People are the Most Valuable Resource**	**Continuous Improvement as a Way of Life**	**Gemba Focused**
Safety • 100% Safe • Zero Incidents	How many customers have we harmed today?	How many employees have we harmed today? • Physically • Mentally • Emotionally	How many resources are focused on improving employee and customer safety?	How many exposures to employee risk of injury have we observed in the gemba today? How much time do we spend in the gemba focused on safety?
Quality • 100% Defect-Free	How many product or service defects have we delivered to our customers today?	How often do we ask employees to pass defects along to their internal &/or external customers? How many defects have our employees eliminated today?	How many resources are focused on improving employee and customer quality?	How much time do we spend in the gemba focused on product or service quality?
Delivery • 100% Complete & On Time	How often have we delivered too early or too late to our customers?	How often do employees have what they need & when they need it to deliver complete & on time to their customers?	How many resources are focused on improving employee and customer delivery?	How much time do we spend in the gemba focused on product or service delivery?
Cost • 100% Value-Added • Zero Waste	How much non value-added activity (waste) we do pass along (charge) to our customers?	How much waste do employees struggle with in their daily work? How difficult is it for employees to add value?	How many resources are focused on reducing customer cost?	How much time do we spend in the gemba focused on reducing product or service cost?
Morale • 100% Employee Delight • 100% Customer Delight	What did we do today to delight our employees? What did we do today to delight our customers?	What did we do today to improve employee morale? To what extent do managers treat employees like customers?	How many resources are focused on improving employee and customer morale?	How much time do we spend in the gemba focused on employee and customer morale?

If you are interested to learn more about the grid above, Edward Blackman, a behavioral expert, helps explain the Toyota's Business Value Grid in the Business Science Magazine article titled, "Mythopoeic Company Values.[*]"

The leadership team should review your vision, values, and success measures regularly. You must evaluate every aspect of your vision to ensure it is still relevant. Be careful when making changes! Both big and small changes to your vision can completely transform the direction your organization is heading.

---

[*] Edward Blackman, Mythopoeic Company Values. Business Science Magazine (US: 2020)

Case Study: Company Continuous Improvement Vs. Company Continuous Appearance

So many keep walking, and walking, and walking, but never get anywhere. When I started with Company Continuous Appearance, the continuous improvement practices were already in place and I immediately started operating with them. I saw pockets of good work, but I wasn't sure where we were going. During my onboarding time, I sat through some basic continuous improvement classes taught by a so-called lean expert who didn't seem to have much actual experience in continuous improvement application with teams on the operations floor. Rather, he was a degreed engineer who had read a lot of lean books. He was definitely book smart, and he knew his stuff. He created excitement in the room with Japanese terms, a few red and green books, and diagrams on PowerPoint. Despite all of that, however, I still wasn't sure what our overall goal was when I finally arrived in my role. At the time, I didn't understand our True North. I knew we needed a vision. My team was faced with many challenges, and they were quickly getting overwhelmed. They were looking to me for direction. So, as a new leader, I looked to my peers, Darrel and Todd, for guidance. They, too, found themselves without a True North or long-term vision to give them direction.

As I began to understand problems in my area, I asked Todd how the company approached problem solving. He showed me an Excel document in a shared folder. When we opened it, we found three columns titled: Problem, Owner, Due Date. As I began to scroll through the document, I noticed there were many items without owners or due dates. There were over 650 items listed in this document and some of them had past-due dates over twelve months old. As I read through the items, I couldn't find any real direction. It seemed leadership was just throwing every challenge and suggestion into this form and hoping for implementation and direction. On the contrary, however, what was actually happening was that each leader was pulling their teams in different directions. The list of problems was all over the

QUESTION 3

place; some teams were working on chipped paint on railings, while others were focused on machine uptime.

Imagine competing in a rowing competition. You're in a boat with seven other people. The vision is to arrive at the finish line in first place. One rower contributes to the overall vision by working two oars, one in each hand, at the same speed and in unison with the other rowers. When each rower's individual actions are aligned toward the vision, the rowing boat travels in one direct line, toward the finish line. Now imagine each of the eight rowers is rowing in a different direction, in the direction they feel is best for their own position at the given time; one down river, one up river, one toward shore, and yet another without oars in the water, just relaxing and taking in the scenery. If perfection is the finish line, how long will it take this team to arrive? How long

> **When each rower's individual actions are aligned toward the vision, the rowing boat travels in one direct line, toward the finish line.**

will it take this team to even achieve excellence?

At Company Continuous Appearance, we were all rowing in our own directions. Our boat was simply spinning in circles with no clear direction. Sometimes a strong leader like Tammy would start rowing furiously toward the finish line, but by herself, she became exhausted and eventually just gave up.

What do you think happened when a team member brought their supervisor a possible solution, only to have it added to the bottom of a 650-item list for review? Many never heard back. Most likely, the original problem would continue to bother this person every day, and their supervisor might seem oblivious to the issue. Do you think that team member would ever turn in another suggestion? Do you think they would give 100% every day?

Now imagine the supervisor's perspective. Tammy certainly doesn't want to be oblivious to her team's problems. Perhaps when she met with our original team member, she listened intently with every intention of solving the problem. When she arrived back at her office two hours later, however, she tried to open the Excel file to log the solution, but the file was left open and locked by Scott on second shift. She came back the next evening after sending Scott an email and tried again. This time she was able to get in and entered the suggestion into the document the best she could remember. Unsure who to assign it to or what due date to place on it, she left it blank. She figured the continuous improvement team would see it and assign it to the proper person. Six months later, the team member is still waiting to hear back and is now looking for another job. This is a pattern I see all the time.

I attended a meeting with Chris and some of the executives of Company Continuous Appearance one day. While in this meeting, one of the executives asked Chris how he was performing toward the company's long-term vision of 99% on-time delivery. I had been with the company for quite some time and was surprised to hear the term long-term vision. I had never before heard anything about a 99%

QUESTION 3

on-time delivery vision. I remember thinking to myself, *Our delivery status is reviewed each month at the plant meetings and we are usually told whether we are doing well or not, so maybe this long term vision is not something I need to know or be concerned with.*

So Company Continuous Appearance was really suffering a double-whammy. On the floor, because there was no vision spelled out, the team operated as anyone would in the absence of a clear direction, with everybody pulling oars in all different directions at once. Worse yet, plenty of people had given up on improvements because the list became endless and little was ever completed. Meanwhile, at the plant manager level, because Chris had never communicated important objectives such as the 99% on-time delivery goal, he didn't have the rest of the team behind him on it and results suffered.

In contrast, at Company Continuous Improvement, they were already on their lean journey when I hired on. The organization as a whole and each plant had identified their True North. For example, the organization established a True North for Quality as "Zero Defects." The True North of the organization was cascaded down to the team members running lines within each of the plants. During my onboarding, we were taken out to the production floor and partnered with team members. The team members who were doing the value-creating work showed us, with pride, all the amazing lean solutions they had been incorporating in their areas. They proudly presented the company values and how their work was contributing to a shared vision. One team member, Rob, walked me through a solution he had personally implemented which resulted in a reduction of quality errors on one of the production lines. I remember him saying to me, "This solution brought us one step closer to our zero-defect goal." The lightbulb went off for me and the connection was made. Rob not only knew the company's True North, but he was actively engaged in making it happen.

When opportunities arose in Company Continuous Improvement, we always checked back with our True North to determine how much energy we would expend on that situation. If the challenge was keeping us from moving closer to our True North, then we would make that item a priority. When other challenges arose, we didn't ignore them, but the team understood why they would not get the same attention as those in alignment with our long-term vision. Those ideas that were not in alignment would be vetted out on an Impact/Effort Matrix by the team to determine how we would approach them.

	Quick Wins!	Major Projects
IMPACT ↑	High Impact Low Effort	High Impact High Effort
	Fill In Jobs	Thankless Tasks
	Low Impact Low Effort	Low Impact High Effort

DIFFICULTY (EFFORT) →

As a team, we would rank each item on the chart and place the Post-it notes where we felt the item best fit with the impact it would have toward our long-term vision, and with the level of difficulty it would take to implement. We thought about effort as people resources, financial resources, and the time it would take for implementation. By ranking the items together, our team would reach consensus. In this way, each team member can better understand why an idea is or is not being implemented at any given time.

***

Sometimes, when organizations don't realize results right away or difficulties push them off the trail, they give up. When this happens, many organizations tend to blame the continuous improvement initiatives. But when they do, organizations sabotage any future opportunities to implement change and may miss out on the amazing opportunities they might otherwise experience.

Your Call To Action

Have you established your organizational vision, and do your team members know their purpose? Maybe you have an organizational vision but your team is not aligned or doesn't know how they can impact it. Create a challenge to meet your desired state.

The organization's purpose should engage its people. It should drive all daily activity for the organization. A vision gives a clear and specific picture of what the organization would look like if they met or achieved this purpose at some time in the future. Begin by creating a long-term vision (True North). Second, create a communication plan for your vision. Finally, determine how to align team member behaviors to the vision. What values are important to support the vision and how will you measure success? Create challenge questions that intersect the two areas.

Determine how you can make your vision visible to your entire organization. Consider posting it where everyone can see it daily and include it in all key messages, as well as in all internal and external communications.

How often should the leadership team review your vision and values? You must evaluate every aspect of your vision to ensure it is still relevant.

Answer all questions using the following abbreviations:

1=No 2=Sometimes 3=Mostly 4=Yes/Always

ARE YOU PURSUING PERFECTION?	
1. Does your organization have a long term vision?	
2. Does everyone know the long term vision?	
3. Do people know how their work personally contributes to the vision?	
4. Is the vision message consistent?	
5. Do you have a formal marketing campaign to communicate your vision?	
QUESTION 3 TOTAL	

Transfer your total to the full assessment at the end of the book. Compare totals to establish a priority.

QUESTION 4

How Stable Are You Today?

> **"Without standards, there can be no Kaizen."**
>
> ~Taichi Ohno, Engineer and Manager at the Toyota Production Company

Some companies are struggling to create excitement and energy within their teams around the idea of change. As I mentioned in Question 1 (Are You Content?), they seem to be content with the status quo. Is this dangerous? The answer is yes...and no.

We can th<u>in</u>k of the status quo as the current or existing state or condition. Taichi Ohno, considered to be the father of the Toyota Production System, said, "Progress cannot be generated when we are satisfied with existing situations," but he also said, "Without standards, there can be no Kaizen[*]." In this second statement, he meant that we must embrace the status quo by standardizing our processes. Do these statements seem a little contradictory? Often, I hear people struggle with how to reconcile the topics of discontentment and standardization. Let me explain.

Many companies live in a state of chaos and instability. They try to

---

[*] "Kaizen means improvement. Moreover, it means continuing improvement in personal life, home life, social life, and working life. When applied to the workplace kaizen means continuing improvement involving everyone – managers and workers alike." Masaaki Imai, Founder of Kaizen Institute

begin improving while still in this chaos state. But how will you ever really know that you are getting better if you have no idea where you are starting? The instability of their operations and leadership causes things to fall apart.

> **But how will you ever really know that you are getting better if you have no idea where you are starting?**

If your operation is in total chaos, then you need to stabilize before you can improve. Stability is necessary in any transformation process. When it comes to stability, we are aiming for low variation and high quality. So how do we create low variation? Standards. If everyone is doing things differently, then there will be high variation and a greater potential for chaos. When we create a standard way of doing things, train our team to the standard, and establish accountability to those standards, the result is low variation and high quality.

Developing and following standardized work helps create the stability needed for any organization to begin their improvement journey.

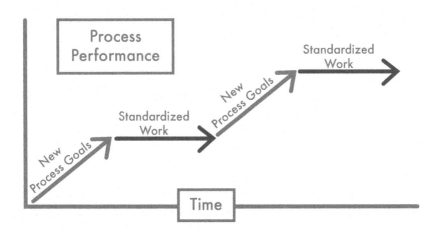

Mark S. Doman, a professor in lean studies at Oakland University, says:

AVOIDING THE CONTINUOUS APPEARANCE TRAP

"As I have told my students many times, the least sexy part of lean is standardized work. But standardized work is the linchpin of the lean system. Standardized work is the playbook. When the play is called for a post pattern over the middle, the quarterback expects the receiver to break inside and not decide to run a fly pattern because it's the fastest way to the end zone. Team members can't be designing and running their own plays because they want to take a shortcut, or they don't like the play called. That's not teamwork. That's not lean."

Begin by choosing one small process and observe the process at least ten times. Ask yourself these five questions:

1. Do we have documented standards visually displayed in work areas?

In addition to leader standard work, if you don't have documented standards visually displayed in your work areas, then you must establish standards in your operations and processes. Establish your current best way of doing things. Work together to analyze the current process, make any necessary improvements, and document the new standard work. The people closest to the work should be the ones creating the standard work. Make it visual and post it at the place where the work is being done.

> **The people closest to the work should be the ones creating the standard work.**

Instead of developing long documents with multiple pages, which can be hard for people to read and understand, you might begin by creating guidelines that can be documented in a simple way. That doesn't mean you may not still have more detailed instructions kept somewhere accessible when they are needed. Your displayed standard work and the training associated with it should answer four questions:

- Who does what?
- When do you do it and how often (to meet customer demand)?
- How do you do it?
- Why do you do it that way?

2. Not all work needs to be standardized. So how do you know what should be standardized?

When deciding if standard work is needed for a job, staff should ask themselves why the steps in the process would benefit from consistency and/or documentation. If the answer is that they wouldn't, standard work isn't going to be helpful in that situation.

Remember that your processes are not standardized just because you have instructions, written by some process engineer, hanging on a wall near the workstations or, even worse, in a computer system. Describing the steps of the process is certainly a good start but is not enough.

3. Are team members trained to those standards, and are they following the standards?

> **They must understand what is expected and why the expectations exist.**

Training for new hires should include classroom time as well as one-on-one coaching and mentorship. You must give adequate time for new hires to learn the standards; they must understand what is expected and why the expectations exist. Audit regularly to assure compliance to the standards by both new hires and existing employees.

4. What actions are taken when there is a deviation from the standards?

When leaders are engaged properly in value-creating work and daily management, deviations from the standard are identified quickly. Everybody involved in the process becomes equally responsible for quickly correcting the problem and restoring the expected level of performance. Create an environment where hiding problems is neither acceptable nor possible. Team members must be trained and feel comfortable with exposing problems, effectively solving them, asking for help and getting it whenever necessary.

5. How can we improve and find process gains?

Like leader standard work, operations and process standard work should be a living document. Update standard work regularly as improvements are made. Team members should feel safe to question every element of a process and seek out ways to improve. For each element of standard work, team members should ask themselves: What is the purpose of this element? Why is it necessary? Am I the right person? Is the timing correct? How should it be done? Team members should be given adequate time to question and experiment to determine if they can eliminate, combine, rearrange or simplify elements of standard work. When controlled experiments prove a better way of doing things, individuals can agree to update standard work and retrain the rest of the team. When updates are made to a process, standard work should be updated. New hires should always be trained to the most

> **Team members should be given adequate time to question and experiment to determine if they can eliminate, combine, rearrange or simplify elements of standard work.**

updated standard work.

To illustrate this process further, imagine your current process of getting ready for work.

Imagine that finding your purse or wallet normally takes you sixty seconds. To streamline this, perhaps you could consider placing it next to your keys instead. If it takes twelve minutes to get dressed in the morning because you need to pick what you are going to wear, how about laying out your clothes on a chair the night before? You could also set timers on appliances, so your to-go coffee is ready as you are walking out the door. Before you know it, you'll have saved a whole bunch of minutes!

If this were the case, wouldn't you want to update the way you do things and save yourself a whole bunch of minutes every day, rather than on just one occasion? Update your standard process to match the new process. Then take the time to stabilize the process. Take time to ensure that you get in the habit of leaving your purse near the keys, setting your clothes out the night before, and setting the timer on your coffee. Once that one is stable, look for other opportunities to improve on the new process!

Case Study: Company Continuous Improvement vs. Company Continuous Appearance

> *"Employee turnover is through the roof! It seems like we're losing good talent daily."*

This was the first statement made to me by the manager of one of the service centers at Company Continuous Appearance. He went on to explain the challenge:

> *"Things aren't like they used to be. In the past, people were content to stay and work for one company. They felt pride to be part of a team. Today, they leave when the wind changes. There are many other service centers in this area who pay*

really well. If people aren't happy, they just get up and walk out. There is no commitment. No dedication to the team. This instability causes many problems for us. We commit so many resources to hiring and training and cannot keep up with our primary work."

One of the biggest pain points for Company Continuous Appearance was managing employee turnover. It cost money to recruit, hire, onboard, and train a new employee. So when that same employee turned around and quit six months later, most of those efforts were lost. This negatively impacted the company's bottom line, not to mention the enormous headaches it caused for the team.

There was nothing more frustrating for the service center trainers than to invest time and effort into someone just to have them not show up the next week. What a waste!

Similar struggles happened at the leadership level. Company Continuous Appearance allowed leaders to bring in their own way of doing things and intentionally moved leaders around regularly. Most leaders did not stay in a role longer than one or two years. This constant changing of the guard with no real consistency in management strategy left the teams in complete confusion.

After working for so long in an environment without standards, most people at Company Continuous Appearance had become numb to the instability and chaos around them. Dealing with problems created by a lack of standards had become the norm. New employees, however, saw and felt the chaos very quickly. It was difficult for new employees to understand expectations when they were trained to do the same job five different ways depending on who they talked to.

While at Company Continuous Appearance, I noticed there was never any standard work posted visually in work areas. When I asked where I could find their work instructions, they would bring me to one of the shared computers centrally located between ten to fifteen other workstations. Sometimes we could find the standard work, which was

QUESTION 4

outdated at times, and there were times we could not find anything. Some team members would bring me to a cabinet and pull out a large book with hundreds of pages of worthless information, and direct me to "look through here." When I asked why their standard work wasn't visually posted or easily accessible, they told me that due to certain quality standards, all documents needed to be controlled and they didn't have the resources to approve, review, or identify revision status, so the company made the decision to eliminate all posted documents from public sight. New employees were being trained by someone who was teaching the method they felt was the best, whether that was the same method on standard work or not; no one really knew. The result was that people were being trained differently for the same tasks. Some trainers skipped steps they felt were not important and others added steps they thought were necessary. Because there were no standards posted, they were never updated when the team tried to make improvements and nothing stuck.

On the other hand, Company Continuous Improvement made the decision to make standard work visible and posted at every workstation. They allocated the appropriate resources and trained certain team members to maintain proper control of all documents on the production floor. Standard work audits were added to leader standard work, and any time team members found and agreed upon a better way to do something, they were empowered to update standard work and retrain team members to the new standard.

Company Continuous Improvement was also committed to hiring or promoting the right leadership into the right roles and then allowing them adequate time to ensure stability. They were never bringing in a new way of doing things. They were developed internally to the way Company Continuous Improvement did things. When a leader moved to a new location, they simply picked up where the last leader left off and usually there was adequate overlap between the leaders.

Your Call To Action

If your processes and your leadership are not stable then you must ask yourself what steps are necessary to get there. Begin experimenting with standard work and work instructions. Determine your one best way of doing things and be sure everyone is trained and following the new standards. Remember, your standard work and the training associated with it should answer four questions:

Who does what?

When do you do it and how often (to meet customer demand)?

How do you do it?

Why do you do it that way?

Standard work should be visually displayed in your work areas. Post it at the place where the work is being done.

Answer all questions using the following abbreviations:

1=No 2=Sometimes 3=Mostly 4=Yes/Always

HOW STABLE ARE YOU TODAY?	
1. Is there stability in your leadership team?	
2. Is your leadership communicating a stable message?	
3. Are you using standardization to sustain improvement gains?	
4. Do you have standard work displayed visually?	
5. Are you updating your standard work as improvements are made?	
QUESTION 4 TOTAL	

Transfer your total to the full assessment at the end of the book. Compare totals to establish a priority.

QUESTION 5

Who's Accountable?

> **"The only way to get people to care...is to show them you care about THEM!!"**
>
> ~Karyn Ross, Author of How to Coach for Creativity and Service Excellence, and Coauthor of The Toyota Way to Service Excellence

Many times I hear leaders say, "We need to hold our employees accountable!" And by that they mean: blame. So many leaders think that accountability means they need to find someone to point a finger at. But accountability is not something you can force. Ideally, your team should decide to accept accountability, and it should be shared. Dr. W. Edwards Deming, the legendary continuous improvement guru who helped rebuild Japan after WWII, said, "Fix the process, not the people." But how do leaders create an environment where the focus is on the process, and where people can decide to be accountable?

Leaders need to place their focus first on the process. They must ask themselves what is broken in the process or the system before turning to their people. Does that mean people don't need to be accountable? Not at all.

Accountability is really a behavior. When I was in the Marine Corps, I learned that for Marines to be accountable, the Marine Corps does two things. First, it trains them to be disciplined and not to accept lack of discipline. Second, they are held responsible, along with their leadership, when they don't follow that guideline.

Marines continuously train to employ discipline through classroom-based discussion sessions and high-intensity simulation training. These trainings test Marines individually and as part of a team. Lack of discipline is never accepted, and is addressed immediately through coaching or, when necessary, constructive discipline.

The higher the rank of the Marine, the higher the standard of discipline. Established standards are not treated as guidelines or suggestions; they are treated as the law. Marines are placed in train-the-trainer positions when considered for certain promotions and cannot be promoted without rising to meet these established standards.

> **Established standards are not treated as guidelines or suggestions, they are treated as the law.**

So how does this relate to you? Discipline starts at the top with accountability. While a leader might be frustrated with the lack of follow-through, action, or employees' attention to detail, their employees, on the other hand, are often complaining about lack of clear priorities, training, expectations, and support; this is part of the process! And leaders are responsible to ensure the process is sound. In addition to this, you must also consider how you're developing discipline within your employees. This is an intentional act; it won't just happen on its own.

Imagine a large cargo ship in the ocean. Some cargo ships are over 1,200 feet long and none of them will turn immediately. So if a captain wants to turn the ship 90 degrees, they must plan ahead, collaborating with their entire crew. From the time the captain commits to the 90-degree turn, it takes 0.373 nautical miles to complete; that's over seven football fields! Each crew member is responsible for their actions during the maneuver. In fact, when a ship is first launched, the ship's crew conducts many trial maneuvers before heading out to open water. If any team member doesn't fulfill their part of the process, the ship could go off course.

Who should be accountable for holding the course, then? The captain? Or the crew?

While accountability starts at the top, both the captain and the crew must share overall accountability. In his blog titled, *Lean, Deming, and Accountability*[*], Mark Graban gives senior leaders five focus areas for creating a culture of accountability through their own actions:

1. *C-level executives demonstrate the right behaviors (always, and I mean ALWAYS, following hand hygiene protocols when entering a unit or a room)*

2. *C-level executives can hold VPs accountable for behaviors (which includes learning how to remove barriers and look at systemic factors)*

3. *VPs can hold Directors accountable*

4. *Directors can hold Managers accountable*

5. *Managers can hold Staff accountable (working together to solve systemic problems, not just blaming and punishing)*

The right structure must be in place to create the right environment for employees to choose accountability:

- Work standards: Defining how work gets done or what is expected

- Visual controls: Something that monitors actual vs. expected

---

[*] Mark Graban, Published December 5, 2013: https://www.leanblog.org/2013/12/lean-deming-and-accountability/

- Leader standard work: Your personal accountability document, the link between standard and visual controls

- Feedback accountability process: Monitoring and measuring system

- Structured Problem Solving: The tools and techniques used to address the gaps, learn as much as you can as fast as you can, and create and improve standards

Leading change is like sailing a large cargo ship in the ocean. It takes time, a lot of hard work, and an accountable crew collaborating effectively to turn the ship! Whether you come from a large corporate entity or a small non-profit organization, change will not happen without accountability.

***

In *The Tipping Point*[*], Malcolm Gladwell discusses how small actions at the right time, in the right place, and with the right people can create a tipping point. When a few trailblazing change agents come together and align with one powerful cause, they can trigger a chain reaction that will spread through the entire organization!

> **When a few trailblazing change-agents come together and align with one powerful cause, they can trigger a chain reaction that will spread through the entire organization!**

One suggestion to promote accountability throughout the organization is to establish a team of change agents who can become cheerleaders for the change efforts.

This group of people becomes a team of ever-learning teachers who

---
[*] Malcolm Gladwell, The Tipping Point (Boston: Little, Brown, 2000)

AVOIDING THE CONTINUOUS APPEARANCE TRAP

practice what they preach, and bravely act as the proverbial thorn in management's side. To begin, consider experimenting with a Promotion Officer who will be accountable to lead, facilitate, and maintain daily management and daily improvement for the change agent team and for the company.

Positive promotion of the change efforts is only one small piece of establishing accountability throughout the organization. Accountability also needs to be communicated clearly.

When I was serving in the military, I learned a valuable lesson about communicating organizational strategy and accountability. Napoleon Bonaparte, a French statesman and military leader during the French Revolution, recognized how vital it was to have an enlisted soldier in the planning process. The lesson of how he acted on this insight is known as Napoleon's Corporal. While creating his army's battle plans and war strategies, Napoleon made sure there was a corporal in the room. Once the plans were complete, he would ask the corporal if he completely understood the plan. If he said, "Yes, sir!" then the general would carry out the plan, knowing it could be cascaded down to the troops on the ground and that they would understand it well enough to execute it and be held accountable. If the corporal did not understand, then the group would continue working on the plan until the corporal understood it.

Establishing a True North and then cascading that True North through the organization effectively can be difficult. You must have a system to assure all the "corporals" know what to do and can be accountable for it! One of the principles of a good strategic plan is to include everyone in the organization in the process.

> **One of the principles of a good strategic plan is to include everyone in the organization in the process.**

of a good strategic plan is to include everyone in the organization in the process. Doing so will result in creating a dynamic, creative business environment.

Case Study: Company Continuous Improvement Vs. Company Continuous Appearance

Using an empowerment continuum chart* can help gauge the team's accountability and readiness for change. I was fortunate to be able to introduce this empowerment continuum chart to a plant in Company Continuous Appearance for the first time. Now, Company Continuous Improvement uses this chart for each team on an annual basis. The empowerment continuum begins with complete respect for the people on the team. After posting the continuum on the wall in a conference room, I met with each team member to ask them three questions: Where were we three years ago? Where are we today? Where do you want to be?

After asking each question, I had them place a colored sticker on the continuum to signify their answer. I used a different color for each shift group, and for leadership. The results were extraordinary!

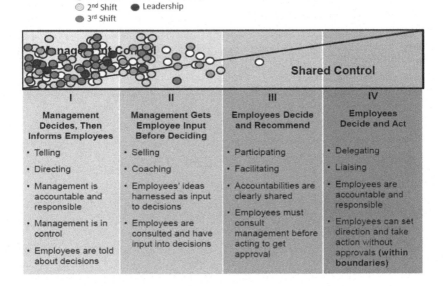

---

* Ingrid Bens, Facilitating With Ease (US: Wiley, 2017)

AVOIDING THE CONTINUOUS APPEARANCE TRAP

Where are we today?

○ 1st Shift　◐ Floor Leadership
◔ 2nd Shift　● Leadership
● 3rd Shift

I	II	III	IV
Management Decides, Then Informs Employees	**Management Gets Employee Input Before Deciding**	**Employees Decide and Recommend**	**Employees Decide and Act**
• Telling	• Selling	• Participating	• Delegating
• Directing	• Coaching	• Facilitating	• Liaising
• Management is accountable and responsible	• Employees' ideas harnessed as input to decisions	• Accountabilities are clearly shared	• Employees are accountable and responsible
• Management is in control	• Employees are consulted and have input into decisions	• Employees must consult management before acting to get approval	• Employees can set direction and take action without approvals (within boundaries)
• Employees are told about decisions			

Where would you like us to be?

○ 1st Shift　◐ Floor Leadership
◔ 2nd Shift　● Leadership
● 3rd Shift

I	II	III	IV
Management Decides, Then Informs Employees	**Management Gets Employee Input Before Deciding**	**Employees Decide and Recommend**	**Employees Decide and Act**
• Telling	• Selling	• Participating	• Delegating
• Directing	• Coaching	• Facilitating	• Liaising
• Management is accountable and responsible	• Employees' ideas harnessed as input to decisions	• Accountabilities are clearly shared	• Employees are accountable and responsible
• Management is in control	• Employees are consulted and have input into decisions	• Employees must consult management before acting to get approval	• Employees can set direction and take action without approvals (within boundaries)
• Employees are told about decisions			

QUESTION 5

In addition to gauging accountability and readiness for change, this exercise can help teams examine what types of change would be valuable. For example, when I asked, "Where are we today?" the third-shift supervisor felt his employees had the freedom to recommend, decide, and even set direction at times without approval. However, when we looked at the data provided by his team, they felt management was in complete control, making all decisions without any input from them. After digging deeper, we found that on this team, the turnover rate was much higher and the rate of improvement suggestions received was much lower than the other shifts. Could this be a result of lower empowerment and accountability? Absolutely.

The data is also telling us that this team is asking to participate more in the decision-making process. In the past three years, team members have become more involved in making decisions and would like more involvement in the future.

In Company Continuous Appearance, all decisions were made by management and management was completely accountable for the results. In fact, there was one scheduled management meeting each week; this was an all-hands, mandatory meeting for all supervisors and manufacturing managers to meet with Chris, the plant manager. During this all-hands meeting, Chris would make decisions for the team. All questions, suggestions, and proposed changes were presented to him, and he would give approval or no-approval decisions. Outside this meeting, very few decisions were made.

Things are quite different at Company Continuous Improvement. At all levels of the organization, team members of Company Continuous Improvement receive "High Performance Team" training. At the very first meeting of this training process, all employees hear the same story of a NASA janitor. During a visit to the NASA space center in 1962, President John F. Kennedy noticed a janitor carrying a broom. He interrupted his tour, walked over to the man, and said, "Hi, I'm Jack Kennedy. What are you doing?"

AVOIDING THE CONTINUOUS APPEARANCE TRAP

"Well, Mr. President," the janitor responded, "I'm helping put a man on the moon."

To most people, this janitor was just cleaning the building. But in the more mythic, larger story unfolding around him, he was helping to make history.

After telling this story, Company Continuous Improvement offers a deep dive into the company's mission statement and True North vision. Each team member is given clear expectations and asked to commit and become accountable to something bigger than themselves. Every job is important and helps achieve the mission. They don't just say it—they believe it and they live it.

While at Company Continuous Improvement, each team member was part of a high-performing team creating change and improvements for their area. Team members had the freedom to experiment and make decisions, within boundaries, and to include communication with the

> **Each team member is given clear expectations and asked to commit and become accountable to something bigger than themselves.**

rest of the team prior to, during, and after improvement experiments. Dave would even give the teams a spending budget for improvements; as long as they stayed within the boundaries, they didn't need to come back to him for permission to spend money on making improvements. They were accountable for these decisions. If experiments proved a better way of doing things and did not compromise safety or quality, they were implemented, standard work was updated, teams were trained as needed, and each team member was off to their next experiment.

QUESTION 5

Your Call To Action

How does your company define accountability today? You may need to start here. Accountability doesn't mean blaming people. Accountability must start with executive leadership, but it is the responsibility of everyone in the organization.

Accountability must be clearly communicated throughout the entire organization. Challenge your team to make your communication visual. Use tools and techniques like work standards, visual controls, leader standard work, feedback accountability processes, and structured problem solving to promote a culture of continuous improvement.

Answer all questions using the following abbreviations:

1=No 2=Sometimes 3=Mostly 4=Yes/Always

WHO'S ACCOUNTABLE?	
1. Do you focus on the process and not on blaming people?	
2. Are team members given clear priorities, expectations, and support?	
3. Do leaders follow through with providing proper support to team members?	
4. Do leaders and members share accountability?	
5. Is accountability discussed and communicated throughout the organization regularly?	
QUESTION 5 TOTAL	

Transfer your total to the full assessment at the end of the book. Compare totals to establish a priority.

QUESTION 6

What Are Your Goals?

> "We cannot become what we want to be by remaining what we are."
>
> ~Max DePree,
> American Businessman and Writer

While serving in the military, I was trained in military planning and decision making. Military officers make decisions about and plan for future operations while they carry out current operations. Many times, at the platoon level, an operation is planned and then initiated almost immediately. At battalion levels, an operation may be planned and initiated within a few hours. At the corps level, several months may be required to plan and initiate a major operation.

During the planning phase, military leaders are looking for options and developing alternatives. When there is a change in the plan information, corresponding changes must be made to the plan.

Have you ever heard the saying, "No battle plan survives first contact with the enemy?"

The ability to make appropriate changes in decisions and plans requires a certain flexibility of mind, a crucial trait for a good leader. Anticipate change. To avoid surprises, think of as many what-ifs as you can. Prepare for them. Adjust ahead of time, if possible, and have contingency plans ready to counteract events that might endanger

QUESTION 6

> The ability to make appropriate changes in decisions and plans requires a certain flexibility of mind, a crucial trait for a good leader.

your mission's accomplishment.

Outside the military, this is known as a Failure Modes and Effects Analysis (FMEA). An FMEA is a systematic, proactive method for evaluating a process to identify where and how it might fail and to assess the relative impact of different failures, in order to identify the parts of the process that are most in need of change and/or to prepare contingency plans. We use FMEA to evaluate processes for possible failures and to prevent them by correcting the processes proactively rather than reacting to adverse events after failures have occurred.

Personal and organizational goal setting is no different than mission or objective planning in the military. All you need is a set of clear objectives that are well defined, measurable, realistic, and time-driven.

Taking into consideration the possibility of adjusting goals on the fly as circumstances change, you must establish a plan to begin. You can use a simple process called SMART goal setting for writing down your goals that will help you hit your targets. Goals need to be measurable. How will you know you are improving if you don't measure it? Ownership should be assigned to one person who has the passion to exceed your expectations. While this person may be assigned ownership, that doesn't mean they are the only one working on that goal. Delegation will be an important quality for this owner.

> **S in SMART is to be Specific.** This means to state exactly what you want to accomplish.
>
> **M in SMART is for Measurable.** How is the information measured for evaluation?

A in SMART is for Attainable. We want to challenge ourselves but we also don't want the team to be defeated because the goal is unattainable.

R in SMART is for Relevant. The goal needs to have a link to our higher-level goals. What organizational goal does this impact?

T in SMART is Time-Bound. There must be a date in which the goal is expected to be resolved so make it realistic. Without a date it is very easy to push this process aside while focusing on other things.

When determining a quantifiable target, leaders must never just pull a number out the air or use a number they feel is a good fit. Leaders should use real data and historical comparisons to choose a target goal that is realistic, and then provide a realistic stretch for the team.

Success should not be measured by hit or miss. As I mentioned in Question 1, a red miss doesn't mean you failed. It means there is opportunity. However, teams can get discouraged when they make great progress on a goal only to fall short on a metric and receive no credit for improvements. If the goal was created based on real data and historical comparisons to make it realistic, yet something out of the ordinary intervened to disrupt the efforts, then leaders should feel comfortable changing the goal during one of their short-cycle goal-setting sessions. Communicating why the goal was changed is important. Or if leaders want to keep the same goal, then they should offer clear communication around why there was a miss, and not place blame on the company's people. The team should still celebrate their many accomplishments on their journey toward meeting the goal. The ability to change a goal, or even throw out a goal that is no longer applicable due to unforeseen changes in the business, promotes a positive impact on our journey toward True North.

During the Battle of la Drang on November 14, 1965, Lieutenant General Hal Moore thought he had the best tactical plan to beat his

QUESTION 6

adversary. He studied the data and communicated clear goals to his team. They trained extensively to assure they had the proper skills to meet the goals. But when they arrived at the battlefield, they were overrun by more soldiers than Moore had anticipated. As the sun went down on his men that night, Moore was distraught by the many casualties. But he did not blame himself or his men. Rather, he spent the evening thanking each of his men for the hard work they put in. While they mourned their lost soldiers, they celebrated the small accomplishments they achieved together that day. Moore reassessed the situation with his leadership team and top generals back in the States, and they adjusted their tactical plan—resulting in a victory over their adversary.

Like Lieutenant General Moore, leaders need to be in constant communication with their team. All results and status reports on tactical goals should be fed back up the tiers of the organization. This ensures a closed-loop system is in place, allowing top management to review the progress of the tactical operations, and adjust their higher-level goals and tactics accordingly.

How can you borrow from these military insights? Let's talk about how you can set up your organization for success in developing the right tactical goals to align with your long-term vision. In Question 3, we discussed the importance of developing your True North, a long-term vision to help direct decision making. In Question 5, you learned about Napoleon's corporal and communicating accountability throughout the organization. In Question 6, we're building on both of these topics as we begin to develop the right tactical goals to align with your long-term vision.

First, you'll need to establish organizational goals, also known as breakthrough objectives. I always begin this process by completing a SWOT* (Strengths, Weaknesses, Opportunities, Threats) Analysis with the executive/senior leadership team. Every SWOT Analysis should

---

* SWOT is a strategic planning technique used to help a person or organization identify strengths, weaknesses, opportunities, and threats related to business competition or project planning.

consider your True North and should be centered on providing value to your customers. Use the results on the SWOT Analysis to help identify your breakthrough objectives. These objectives are three- to five-year goals and should also be in direct alignment with your True North. Try to limit your organizational goals to no more than five so your company can stay focused. Next, the leadership team should develop their annual organizational goals. Remember Napoleon's corporal? You may want to have some mid-managers in the room as part of this process. Where do you want the organization to be one year from now? These one-year goals need to be in alignment with and have a clear connection to the breakthrough objectives.

Finally, it's time to develop the tactical plan to achieve the annual organizational goals. The mid-management team should drive this portion of the goal planning process; I suggest including some team leaders and other key team members in this step of the process too. To create the best tactical plan, managers should meet with their staff to review the organizational goals and to decide how they can best support these objectives. If each layer of management ensures their tactical goals are aligned, the goals will cascade to every team member at every level, meeting the needs of the business. If not, your team will waste precious resources on activities that are good but not great.

> **To create the best tactical plan, managers should meet with their staff to review the organizational goals and to decide how they can best support these objectives.**

A sound strategy development process should enable a company to create and adapt strategy quickly and iteratively, as well as to allocate the proper resources in changing environments. While we are creating one-year goals here, we will also need to break these down even

QUESTION 6

further to quarterly and even shorter goal-setting cycles; we use 90-day cycles. As I mentioned before, leaders need the freedom to adjust goals to meet business needs in an ever-changing environment. Leaders should consider developing alternatives up front to prepare for change. Keeping these alternatives aligned with the organizational goals is key.

Company Continuous Improvement vs. Company Continuous Appearance

As I mentioned in Question 3, Company Continuous Appearance had established some True North objectives, like 99% on-time delivery. However, that long-term vision was not communicated well to the rest of the organization. The goals we were setting were not in clear alignment with the overall organizational direction. Each year, plant managers created annual plant-level KPIs; goals were set by increasing over some percentage from the previous year's goal. Managers were also responsible for creating personal goals for each of their leaders, which were supposed to align with the annual plant goals.

At Company Continuous Appearance, we were told that promotions were based on our ability to meet the annual goals we created with our manager. Usually, I would get an email from Chris that said something like this:

Usually this email came out in October or November, when annual reviews were due to be given in November. Sometimes, if Chris was behind, he wouldn't even ask for goals. He would just input some fake goals with "xxx" entered into the measurement section of the system. He told me we could update the goals later.

Remember, we were told promotions were based on us meeting or not meeting these goals. How do you think this made us feel when we didn't receive clear direction on goals, and sometimes weren't even given goals until later in the year? Goals were a joke.

After a few years of working my butt off to meet our plant KPIs and my personal goals (if I had them), I learned that promotions were not based on meeting goals at all. Rather, they were based on who you knew and how well you could network. Executive leaders would meet and discuss review ratings and promotions. Those leaders who did a good job networking with executive leaders and simply did what they were told, received higher marks on their reviews and eventually were promoted.

Professor Fred Luthans of the University of Nebraska published a study[*] comparing "successful" managers to "effective" managers. He found that successful managers get promoted more rapidly. These managers became successful by networking and politicking. On the contrary, effective managers, who were not being promoted rapidly, spent more time building their units and developing their people. Luthans found that organizations were promoting the wrong people!

This is exactly what was happening at Company Continuous Appearance. Once they settled into a plant manager role or other senior role, these managers no longer felt an obligation to the people on the production floor. Rather, they were consumed with politics, conference room meetings, and one-on-one office meetings with other executives to discuss the evening's golf league. The organization created multiple layers of mid-management in hopes that someone

---

[*] F. Luthans; The Academy of Management Executive, Vol. 2, No. 2 (May, 1988), pp. 127-132

QUESTION 6

would take care of meeting the goals for the organization.

Meanwhile, while Company Continuous Improvement was not perfect, they were diligent to ensure that everyone in the organization understood the connection between their personal work, annual goals, breakthrough goals, and their True North. As a manager, I was involved in setting my goals and the goals for my team. We were mandated to communicate how meeting our personal goals would bring us closer to meeting our organizational goals. We even had to turn in a report for improvement activities to show bottom-line and KPI connections. Using a matrix like the one below, we worked together to make sure our goals were aligned and priorities were set.

				IMPROVEMENT INITIATIVE 3				●	●		
	●	●		IMPROVEMENT INITIATIVE 3		●			●		
●		●		IMPROVEMENT INITIATIVE 2	●				●		●
●	●	●		IMPROVEMENT INITIATIVE 1	●			●		●	●
ANNUAL OBJECTIVES 1	ANNUAL OBJECTIVES 2	ANNUAL OBJECTIVES 3	ANNUAL OBJECTIVES 4	IMPROVEMENT INITIATIVE / ANNUAL OBJECTIVES / IMPROVEMENT TARGETS (KPI) / STRATEGIC OBJECTIVES 3-5 YEARS	IMPROVEMENT TARGET 1	IMPROVEMENT TARGET 2	IMPROVEMENT TARGET 3	IMPROVEMENT TARGET 4	PERSON A	PERSON B	PERSON C	PERSON D

At the plant level, we reviewed our annual goals quarterly. At the value stream level, we reviewed our quarterly goals weekly. At the functional process area level, we reviewed our goals and priorities daily. If special circumstances arose, the teams were comfortable with adjusting their goals if necessary. A closed-loop system assured communication of any adjustments at all levels. The team felt empowered and knew exactly what was expected. While we celebrated many wins and accomplishments, we also had some tough discussions around missed goals, always knowing why we missed, learning from those situations, and adjusting accordingly to the next goal setting cycle.

Your Call To Action

Begin by creating three- to five-year breakthrough objectives for your organization. Consider this your long-term organizational direction. Align your one-year challenge and objectives. Work together with your team to develop a solid tactical plan with both team and personal goals. Use SMART goals to define your next target condition. Your goals should align with the objectives and have a direct connection to your True North.

Make your goals visual. Consider using an improvement Kata storyboard for leaders. If you are using visual charts, be sure they are updated regularly. Meet around this storyboard at some frequency to discuss any obstacles and make potential adjustments that may need to be made due to special circumstances or learnings.

When goals are missed, celebrate any accomplishments on the journey and be transparent about the misses. Discuss your learnings as a team and adjust accordingly on the next goal-setting cycle.

QUESTION 6

Answer all questions using the following abbreviations:

1=No 2=Sometimes 3=Mostly 4=Yes/Always

WHAT ARE YOUR GOALS?	
1. Do your leaders have a 'flexibility of mind'? Do they plan for and anticipate change?	
2. Are you using SMART Goals?	
3. Does your organization have long term and 1-year goals? Are they aligned?	
4. Are you operating on 90-day or similar goal setting cycles?	
5. Are your short goal setting cycles (tactical plan) aligned with your long-term goals?	
QUESTION 6 TOTAL	

Transfer your total to the full assessment at the end of the book. Compare totals to establish a priority.

QUESTION 7

Is Your Organization Designed to Meet Your Goals?

> "Silo walls between business units that impede cooperation and communication need to come down."
>
> ~Howard Stinger,
> CEO of Sony Corporation

We can think of a silo as any process, business unit, department, management style, management structure, or even employee who cannot (or does not) interact with any other process, system, area, or employee. These entities are less likely to share resources or ideas with other groups, or to welcome suggestions about how they might improve. When we have silos among teams or departments, collaboration in a business culture will be limited, unless collaboration benefits the members of the departments in question. In addition, the members of a silo tend to think alike, which can also impede creativity and out-of-box thinking.

Silos are a serious obstacle to many businesses. Silos typically happen slowly and accidentally, and rarely with the value of the process in mind. Sometimes companies don't realize they have silos and other times it is intentional.

Take a moment to assess your organization. Do you currently operate in department silos or with a silo mentality? If the answer is yes, unless your intent is to not share information, goals, tools, priorities, and processes with other departments, then your organization is not designed to meet your

> "A bad system will beat a good person every time."
> ~ W. Edwards Deming

goals. The problem isn't that people show up to work every day wanting to spend their time on wasteful activities that don't bring value to the customer; they want to collaborate. Yet despite best intentions, as W. Edwards Deming said, "A bad system will beat a good person every time."

My youngest daughter loves puzzles. When she gets a new puzzle, she is always careful to open the box in a way that the cover does not get damaged. Once it's open, she pours out the pieces on the table and begins flipping each piece over so she can see the colors and shapes on each individual piece. She then sets up the cover of the box with the picture of the completed puzzle facing her. This way she can see the whole picture of what the puzzle will be when she completes it as she works on it. Without the clear and complete picture on the box, completing the puzzle would be very difficult.

When you step back and begin to make decisions by looking at the big picture, you are now operating in a value stream mindset. A value stream is the entire collection of activities and/or processes necessary to produce and deliver a product or service. It begins with an event that triggers the flow of value and ends when some value has been delivered—a shipment, customer purchase, or solution deployment. The steps in the middle represent the activities used from start to end. The value stream contains the people who do the value-creating work, the systems they develop or operate, and the flow of information, process steps, and materials (if applicable).

Imagine that the value stream is the puzzle. Each of these activities and process steps is one piece of the puzzle. If we were to look at the cover of the value stream "box," we would see how each of the activities fits together to give us a clear picture of the various flows of value within the value stream, and how the value stream looks as a whole. Identifying and understanding the various flows of value are critical steps for improving organizational performance.

Begin by determining your value streams, the processes that create what your customer is asking for. Every value stream contains many actions (puzzle pieces) that come together to create the result. Take manufacturing an automobile as an example. Within the four walls of an assembly plant, what are all the process steps from ordering materials through to final assembly and shipment of the automobile? Another example is serving a hospital patient. Within the hospital, what are all the process steps from the point the patient steps through the doors until the patient is released? Some organizations may have one value stream, while others may have multiple.

The point here is to eliminate the silo mindset that draws improvement activities to one department and doesn't pay attention to the impact upstream or downstream of the department. All steps in a value stream should collaborate, and decisions should be made together with the entire team rowing in the same direction.

QUESTION 7

There are many ways to make your value stream visible; different examples of process and value stream maps can be found with a quick internet search. However, the real value here is in engaging the entire cross-functional team in a visual mapping exercise that give the team a big picture visual with all the data needed identify the problems.

> **However, the real value here is in engaging the entire cross-functional team in a visual mapping exercise that give the team a "big picture" visual with all the data needed identify the problems.**

Follow these six steps to create a good value stream map:

Step 1: Identify customer requirements and calculate how often, and in what amount of time, you need to deliver the product or service to your customer. Always start with the customer's needs.

Step 2: Identify your main process steps and create blank data collection blocks. You will need to determine what your success metrics are for these data blocks. What data is important to measure?

Step 3: Add arrows for flow. Show the direction work is traveling through the value stream from process step to process step. What needs to happen for the next step to take place?

Step 4: Add inventory (if applicable) and delay queues. Note: Inventory can be pieces of material or number of people.

Step 5: Populate the data boxes. What information is needed

AVOIDING THE CONTINUOUS APPEARANCE TRAP

to identify problems and answer questions the team might have?

Step 6: Draw and calculate your lead-time ladder. How long does it take for one product or service to go through the entire value stream? And how much of that time is value-creating and how much is waste?

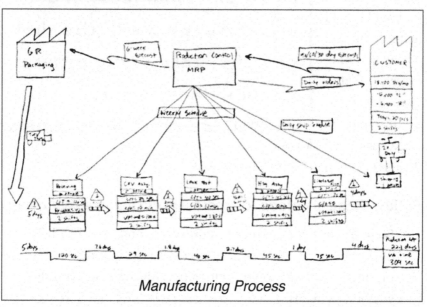
Manufacturing Process

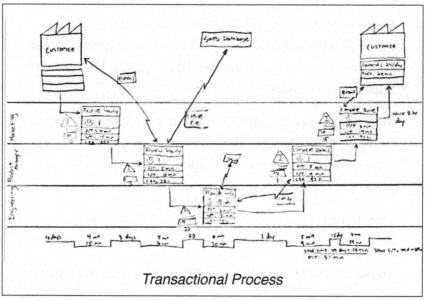
Transactional Process

QUESTION 7

Separating your organization into value streams and creating a current-state value stream map for each value stream is only the first step. Next, you need to identify the delays, problems, and waste in the value stream. Finally, create a future-state value stream with all the delays, problems, and waste eliminated. Now that you know the gap between the two, you can create your roadmap and begin experiments toward your future state.

Case Study: Company Continuous Improvement vs. Company Continuous Appearance

There was a time at Company Continuous Appearance when I was responsible for the stamping department. A second manager was responsible for the weld department, and a third was responsible for the roll form department.

I learned very quickly what was important to Chris. He didn't like when inventory piled up in your area, never wanted the machines to shut down, and would not tolerate a missed shipment. Knowing this, I went to work on what was important to my boss. We did everything we could to keep the lines running. In fact, we made such great progress keeping the lines running that the inventory was no longer piling up before our department. Now, it was piling up *after* our department. This was good for me, because Chris's focus was no longer on me. All focus had shifted to the weld department manager.

Although I'd created a short-term solution for pleasing my boss, I wasn't acting in a way that created sustainable improvements across the value stream for the company. As Mike Rother and John Shook explain in *Learning to See*[*]:

> "You may have already noticed that tracing the value stream for a product family will take you across organizational boundaries in your company. Because companies tend to be organized by departments and functions, instead of by the

---
[*] Rother, M., Shook, J., & Lean Enterprise Institute. (2003). Learning to see: Value stream mapping to create value and eliminate muda

flow of value-creating steps for product families, you often find that no one is responsible for the value stream perspective. It is astoundingly rare to visit a facility and find one person who knows the entire material and information flow for a product (all processes and how each is scheduled). Yet without this, parts of the flow will be left to chance-meaning that individual processing areas will operate in a way that is optimum from their perspective, not the value stream perspective.

To get away from the isolated islands of functionality you need one person with lead responsibility for understanding a product family's value stream and improving it. We call this person a value-stream manager and suggest that in this capacity they report to the top person at your site. This way they will have the power necessary to help change happen."

In other words, although I wanted to avoid my manager's displeasure, I should have found a way to work outside of isolation with the other managers to improve our value stream. More to the point, the company should have offered a value stream manager to facilitate that process for everyone.

> **To get away from the isolated islands of functionality you need one person with lead responsibility for understanding a product family's value stream and improving it.**

While working with Company Continuous Improvement, I had the opportunity to serve as a value stream manager. As a value stream manager, I reported directly to the plant manager and had profit and loss responsibilities over the entire value stream. I was responsible for increasing the value-creating activities and eliminating waste in

QUESTION 7

the overall supply chain from the point a product was ordered to the point Company Continuous Improvement received payment for the product. Upon arriving at Company Continuous Improvement, the product families had already been chosen and the value streams had been in place for quite some time. I assumed leadership over a team consisting of one planner, two engineers, three production supervisors, and 120 indirect team members. As the value stream manager, I was responsible for the following:

Value Stream Manager

Job Description:

Responsibilities:
1. Work with my team to create a current state value stream map of the end-to-end value stream.

2. Conduct an in-depth current state analysis.

3. Prepare an ideal state map showing what the value stream could look like with zero waste and incorporating future state principles.

4. Prepare a future state map showing where the value stream will be in one year.

5. Create a plan to achieve the future state.

6. Develop 90-day high level and detailed level tasks and transformation metrics.

7. Lead the team toward completion of the 90-day tasks, adjusting as needed based on transformation metrics.

8. Create a new current state value stream map and 90-day plan every 90 days until reaching the one-year future state. This future state becomes the new current state and the process starts again.

Your Call To Action

Assess your current operation and determine if you are operating in silos or if you are operating by the flow of value-creating steps. Once you have decided to move to a value-stream-managed organization, begin by gathering any preliminary information. Study historical information about product mix or services offered. Seek out validated data for volume of sales from the previous year. This historical data will help you apply Pareto's 80-20 rule: In most cases, you will find that 20 percent of what you build, or the service you provide, represents 80 percent of your business in a typical year. You may want to consider limiting your value stream activity to this 20 percent.

Identify your value stream(s) by grouping customers and looking at the routing sequences for each product or service. Those customers, products, or services that have similar routing sequences should help you establish distinct families.

Choose one value stream to begin and assign value stream managers. Give your new value stream managers the decision-making capabilities and/or boundaries for making decisions over the entire value stream. Value stream managers need to have experience or be developed as such. Using the six steps I laid out earlier in this chapter, each value stream manager should begin by mapping their value stream.

QUESTION 7

Answer all questions using the following abbreviations:

1=No 2=Sometimes 3=Mostly 4=Yes/Always

IS YOUR ORGANIZATION DESIGNED TO MEET YOUR GOALS?	
1. Is your organization designed to share information, goals, priorities, and processes?	
2. Do the majority of people operate with a big picture (value stream) mindset?	
3. Do you identifiy customer requirements and discuss how to meet demand regularly?	
4. Do the majority of people view your organization or parts of your organization in process steps?	
5. Are you analyzing process steps and/or are you conducting value stream mapping analysis?	
QUESTION 7 TOTAL	

Transfer your total to the full assessment at the end of the book. Compare totals to establish a priority.

QUESTION 8

How Are Your Leaders Behaving?

> "There are three kinds of leaders. Those that tell you what to do. Those that allow you to do what you want. And Lean leaders that come down to the work and help you figure it out."
>
> ~John Shook,
> CEO of the Lean Enterprise Institute

In a survey regarding engagement, Gallup[*] shows the engagement level for managers is at 35%:

> "Day in and day out, managers are tasked with engaging employees, but 51% of managers have essentially 'checked out,' meaning they care little, if at all, about their job and company. And that attitude has direct consequences. A manager's engagement—or lack thereof—affects his or her employees' engagement, creating what Gallup calls the cascade effect."

The way your leaders behave has a direct connection to your culture. These are scary statistics and need to be understood and acted upon if we want to promote the right culture.

While the terms *leadership* and *management* get used interchangeably, they don't mean the same thing. Leadership is about setting a new direction, or vision, for a group to follow. Leaders help themselves, and others, to do the right things. They set direction, build an inspiring

---
[*] https://www.gallup.com/workplace/236552/managers-engaged-jobs.aspx

vision, and create something new. Leadership is about mapping out where you need to go to win as a team, or an organization; it is dynamic, exciting, and inspiring. Management, on the other hand, controls or directs people and resources in a group according to established principles or values. Management involves creating timetables to meet commitments and developing specific action steps. This often requires managers to put some structure to a plan which includes staffing requirements, communications, and delegation of responsibilities.

Every manager is not necessarily a leader, and every leader is not necessarily a manager. I have worked for and with many great leaders who could spearhead an initiative and create engagement and excitement for a vision; however, when it came to time management, communication, and delegation, they were terrible managers. I have also worked with managers who could put together an amazing project plan with proper staffing requirements and the exact action steps necessary for success; however, the team wouldn't follow them. They couldn't figure out how to engage their team members and get them excited about the mission at hand.

A true lean leader is both a leader and a manager. They are developing themselves to practice all of those necessary qualities. As a leader, they can create well-defined vision and strategy. They line up all the relevant stakeholders with this vision and strategy and energize people to achieve the vision, no matter what the obstacle. As a manager, they monitor activities, spot deviations from the plan, and organize solutions. Lean leaders go one step further: They also embrace and champion continuous improvement throughout their organization. They are committed to ensuring activities are value-added, and that people are empowered to solve problems and improve processes.

In the traditional role the leader plans, solves, and acts as the expert, while the lean leader sets the expectation, facilitates root cause analysis, and uses the knowledge of the worker for the expertise.

The best way to define lean leadership is to compare it to traditional leadership. Take a moment and compare the two leadership styles':

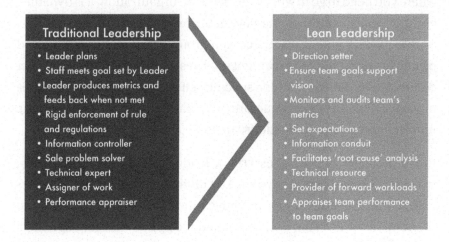

In a lean organization, learning is critical, and is every lean leader's direct responsibility. A strong lean foundation is based on how every person in an organization thinks and behaves. Lean leaders and their team members need a common philosophy, ideas, and principles to effectively communicate with each other. Lean leaders never place their team members into situations to learn the things on their own, no matter their time on the job. Instead, they use questions and real-life experiences to communicate the proper message through direct coaching.

Every good builder knows how to create, but also how to demolish. Lean leaders must build tension and demolish stress. When circumstances are virtually impossible, when the path forward is unclear, and when team members see the gap between their current situation and the ideal state, they may feel tension or stress. But with resources and support from leadership, employees can see a clear path to move forward.

Lean leaders must also eliminate fear of change and contentment with the status quo. Lean culture requires action, experimentation, and a new way of thinking, all of which involve risk. Learning occurs when employees leave the comfort zone.

QUESTION 8

Finally, lean leaders must lead through visible, active participation, not simply by declaring the importance of lean from a conference room or corner office. When *all* leaders participate in or lead waste walks, coach problem solving sessions, and ask operators for their knowledge, employees understand the importance of lean. Through active participation, leaders observe how lean is understood and applied.

***

Dr. Jeffrey Liker's Lean Leadership Development Model[*] will help you break through development plateaus and create a sustainable future for lean thinking in your enterprise. When leaders adopt this model as their system and way of managing, amazing things will begin to happen. The first area of development for leaders is to commit to self-development. The second is to coach and develop others. The third is to support daily Kaizen[**]. And the final development area for leaders is to create vision and align goals.

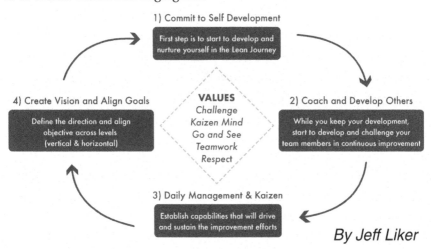

By Jeff Liker

The first of those steps is to Commit to Self-Development. Now, you may have been expecting me to reel off a list of great Lean resources, right? Wrong. Your self-development is about...well, you. My self-

---

[*] Jeffrey Liker and Gary Convis, The Toyota Way to Lean Leadership (US: McGraw-Hill, 2011)
[**] Kaizen focuses on eliminating waste, improving productivity, and achieving sustained continual improvement in targeted activities and processes of an organization.

development needs are going to be different from yours. Everyone is starting from a different point depending on their background and life experiences. Remember that you cannot begin to develop your leadership skills if you are struggling with the security of health, work, money, or family. Your basic needs of sleep, relaxation, activity, and exercise are important, and foundational, to developing your leadership skills. This statement is also true for the leaders who work for you.

Here are five steps to managing your personal self-development following the PDCA model. First, create a vision for where you want to be in the future, and why. This will become your personal-development True North. Every decision should then be aligned with this True North. Most of us find it easier to motivate ourselves to learn and improve if we have a purpose in doing so. Your personal vision will give you a clear idea of where you want to be in a few months or years, and why. This is a crucial part of developing this purpose.

Second, you want to *plan* your personal development journey. Once you are clear about where you want to be, you can start planning how to get there. Whom do you need to meet? What books or podcasts should you listen to? What mentors do you need to reach out to, and on what topics? Drawing up a personal development plan is not essential, but it does make the planning process more realistic. I usually create a one-year plan with 90-day PDCA cycles.

Third, you need to carry out your plan. It's time to *do* something! Don't wait to get started. You can adjust as needed. It is often a good idea to keep a record of your personal development.

This is done in the fourth step—the check phase. By writing down key developments in your learning and development when they occur, you will be able to reflect on your successes later. Regular reviews of your personal development plans and activities will ensure that you learn from what you have done.

The last step is to act. Acting on these results is key. It will also ensure

QUESTION 8

that your activities continue to move you towards your goals, and that your goals or vision remain relevant to you.

Now that you understand the importance of self-development, be sure not to skip it. But for now, let's move into step number two, Coaching and Developing Others. How well do you establish boundaries and build trust? This cannot be done from your desk. You need to go to the Gemba—go to where your team members are and spend time with them. Your team should see you and hear from you daily. You should set up a regular cadence of positive and constructive feedback for your team members. A good leader doesn't just TELL. Ask strategic questions to help your team members realize opportunities for improvement themselves and then give them the credit. Ask them to show you how they do their job. Show genuine interest in their work and in their personal lives. Do you know each employee's personal challenges? Do you know their spouse's name? How many kids do they have? You need to genuinely care for the people you work with. They know the difference.

> **Ask strategic questions to help your team members realize opportunities for improvement themselves and then give them the credit.**

Be intentional to challenge the thinking and assumptions of others. You have to be careful with this one because you don't want your team to think you are micromanaging them. Their learning will come through their own mistakes. Allow them to experiment, but challenge strategically with good questions. Help your team members set meaningful goals, hold them accountable, and help remove any roadblocks they may have for successes.

The third step in the Leadership Development Model is Daily Management and Kaizen. The best way to build and sustain a continuous improvement culture is incremental. Daily accountability is key! Do you remember what you read in Questions 2 and 5?

By following your own daily leader standard work, you will begin to solve problems quickly, creatively, and permanently. Collaboration will become a regular occurrence as your coaching and developing of others becomes a regular habit. Personal productivity and time management are important to assure complete success at the end of each day.

The concept of Kaizen is centered around making small changes to get better. In a Kaizen event, we seek to link a small change to a more concentrated set of activities, to drive toward a more aggressive breakthrough.

The fourth step in the Leadership Development Model is to Create Vision and Align Goals. Align all the Kaizen efforts that you might think of as the small pictures to ensure that the right big-picture goals are accomplished. In other words, this is where bottom-up meets top-down. Without guidance and channeling of efforts, Kaizen could lead to chaos: Two interlocking processes could be pursuing Kaizen that takes them into opposite directions. At this stage of development, the leader and the organization are actively involved in what, in Japanese, is called Hoshin Kanri. This method is the process of setting consensus goals for long-term improvement and deciding on the best allocation of efforts and resources to reach those goals.

This is far more than the cascading-goals process that is common in many companies using management by objectives[*]. All companies have plans, goals, and targets. It is rare for leaders to be able to break these down and align their daily efforts in such a way that each work group understands and owns its portion of the big-picture goals and has a clearly defined plan for how it will accomplish them. As a lean <u>leader, you don</u>'t just set goals and targets that people struggle to

[*]Management by objectives, also known as management by results, is a strategic management model that aims to improve the performance of an organization by clearly defining objectives that are agreed to by both management and employees. It was first popularized by Peter Drucker in his 1954 book The Practice of Management.

achieve. Instead, you actively participate in translating those goals into concrete targets for improvement, and coach the skills needed to ensure success.

Case Study: Company Continuous Improvement Vs. Company Continuous Appearance

Leaders at Company Continuous Appearance spent most of their days fire-fighting—that is, constantly engaged in the rapid and immediate response to problems. Many times, these unplanned response needs dragged leaders away from their planned daily activities. Solutions become temporary band-aids that are never really completed, and eventually become the next fire the team would have to deal with in the future.

Darrell and Todd struggled to make one walk-around of the production floor without getting pulled in to help solve a serious problem. Both always seemed to be running around responding the next hot item. When I would ask them, "What does your day look like today?" their response was, "Hard to say. It depends on what fires we will get today." I imagined when Darrell and Todd walked through the front doors each morning, they had a similar feeling to that of an actual firefighter walking into a burning building, with no idea who needed to be saved and whether the building was going to fall on them. The first thing they experienced was like getting hit in the face with a backdraft each morning from Tammy. Every day would start with Tammy updating Darrell and Todd on all the fires she had had throughout the night, and how Darrell and Todd would need to follow up on those items.

I found myself constantly wondering how the team would ever make progress when only key leaders were providing solutions to the problems.

At one point, I had to step in. One day, someone literally ran up to Darrell and me as we were walking the floor and started yelling about a machine being down. I knew right away this was a fire. Darrell's

AVOIDING THE CONTINUOUS APPEARANCE TRAP

normal response was to stop whatever he was doing and immediately deal with that problem. This caused him to sometimes forget about his task at hand or miss important daily activities. With Darrell's permission, I asked the operator what *he* thought we should do. He looked at me a little crazy-like and then looked at Darrell as if to get permission to answer, and he said, "I guess I would clean the rails." I said, "Ok. Clean the rails and let us know if that works." As he left, Darrell turned to me and said, "That won't work...I believe one of the rails is bent." I responded, "That's all right. Because when it doesn't work, your operator will learn something. And maybe he'll learn that the rail is bent and know what to do. All on his own, without having to come get you. You see, every time you solve a problem for your team, you enable them to create fires for you. They begin to rely on you as the one person who can fix things. However, you want them to be the experts who solve the problems. Let them learn. Imagine how much more you could get done."

Darrell had an open mind and over the next few weeks, I watched him start asking his team what they thought, and he began enabling them to experiment, even when he knew the answer.

***

At Company Continuous Improvement, our development of our people started before they were even hired. We avoided standard job interviews. In the beginning of the hiring process, we worked closely with Human Resources to ensure that we would get the right candidates for the interview. Once a candidate was identified for an interview with our team, we would spend time getting to know them and their aspirations. Leaders at Company Continuous Improvement gave EVERY candidate the respect they deserved as a human being. We never rushed an interview. We also introduced each candidate to the team, sometimes in a conference room and sometimes out on the production floor. This was also true for leaders being brought in from the outside—candidates would spend time with the employees they would be managing. We asked those employees to provide feedback before we hired anyone, and we respected their input. We placed the candidates in situations where they would be likely to show their true selves; many times, this happens when you leave the candidate with the team members.

Your Call To Action

Take inventory. Are you ready to develop your leadership skills or do you need to take care of some basic needs first? Do not take this lightly. Many leaders burn out quickly because they don't take the time to stabilize their marriage or home life. Be sure your physiological and psychological needs are being met so you can focus on your leadership capabilities.

What kind of leader are you? Are you the kind of leader that tells others what to do? Are you the kind of leader that allows others to do what they want? Or are you the kind of leader that comes down to the work and helps others figure it out?

What improvements are necessary in developing yourself as a leader? Develop your own PDCA self-development plan and follow it. Find a coach to hold you accountable.

After you have established your own plan, take inventory of the other leaders in your organization. How well do you know your team? You must genuinely care about each one of them and their challenges as a human being. Be sure their basic needs are being met before you begin talking to them about how they can reach their full potential as a leader.

What kind of leaders are they? Are they willing to change? Sit down with each leader and help them develop their own PDCA self-development plan. Become their coach and accountability partner.

Actively participate in translating your teams' goals into concrete targets for improvement, and coach the skills needed to ensure success.

Answer all questions using the following abbreviations:
1=No 2=Sometimes 3=Mostly 4=Yes/Always

HOW ARE YOUR LEADERS BEHAVING?	
1. Is your leadership team engaged?	
2. Are your leaders acting as leaders and managers?	
3. Do your leaders have a formal self-development plan in place?	
4. Are your leaders spending a large amount of time coaching and developing others?	
5. Are all leaders involved in vision casting and goal alignment?	
QUESTION 8 TOTAL	

Transfer your total to the full assessment at the end of the book. Compare totals to establish a priority.

QUESTION 9

How Safe Is It for Your Employees to Fail?

> "Leaders' words and actions set the culture for their organization. Seemingly small choices when it comes to language and behavior can have a big impact in shaping the people-centered culture you want for your organization."
>
> ~Katie Anderson, Author of *Learning to Lead, Leading to Learn*

Captain D. Michael Abrashoff is a former Navy Commander and the author of *It's Your Ship: Management Techniques from the Best Damn Ship in the Navy*[*], a story of organizational transformation and innovative leadership. Abrashoff took command of the worst-performing Navy ship in the Pacific Fleet and made it #1 in twelve months—using the very same crew. In his book, Abrashoff says, "Short of these contingencies, the crew was authorized to make their own decisions..."

Wow! Can you imagine how difficult it must have been for him to hand over decision-making authority to his crew? Do you think he trusted they would make all the right decisions? Absolutely not. In fact, he knew they would make mistakes.

He continues, "Even if those decisions were wrong, I would stand by them. Hopefully, they would learn from their mistakes. And the more responsibility they were given, the more they learned."

---

[*] D.M. Abrashoff, It's Your Ship: Management Techniques from the Best Damn Ship in the Navy (New York: Warner Books, 2002)

QUESTION 9

Do you think Abrashoff's crew felt safe to make decisions? When they made the right decision, the Captain celebrated with the entire crew! When they made the wrong decision, he made sure they learned something. Either way, the crew found success in making their own decisions one way or the other.

Imagine being a new sailor on the worst-performing ship in the Navy. As an eighteen-year-old sailor, you determine a problem with the ship's integrated bridge and navigation system. In the past, if you raised a problem to your Senior Chief, you were told, "There are experts to work on that stuff. Stop complaining and get back to your job!" Needless to say, if left unresolved, a problem like this could lead to a malfunction, a collision, and even potential death of crew members.

When people work in a fear-based culture, they tend to overlook things that should be addressed immediately.

Now imagine being a sailor on the same ship when Captain Abrashoff took command. Abrashoff told his crew that their top priority was the safety and security of his people. But he didn't just say it, he lived it. To embed a mindset of safety takes action, not just words. The Captain would personally inspect workspaces, observe sailors performing their duties, quiz them on protocol, and would participate in safety seminars with his crew. Any sailor could stop any process if they thought safety was being impaired. Any sailor had a direct line to him if they felt their chain of command wasn't sufficiently concerned. And Captain Abrashoff would stand behind them and support them, even if they made a bad decision. The result was only two minor incidents aboard, down from thirty-one in the preceding two years.

***

Companies cannot develop breakthrough processes if they are not willing to encourage risk taking and learn from subsequent mistakes. In traditional work environments, managers are expected to make most decisions and assume all responsibility. How many problems can one manager attend to? If everyone in the organization is waiting for one manager to make a decision, how slow will the decision-making process be? In work environments where managers make all the decisions, employees get frustrated because they are dealing with the same problems over and over again. Managers don't have the time to fully understand every situation and therefore will either not make a decision fast enough or will make a hasty but ill-informed decision that could result in negative results. In contrast, continuous improvement cultures engage everyone in decision-making and responsibility. Imagine how strong the organization would be if everyone was engaged in good root-cause analysis and countermeasure implementation. For everyone to be engaged, however, they need to feel safe to fail.

> In contrast, continuous improvement cultures engage everyone in decision making and responsibility.

When a reporter asked him how it felt to fail a thousand times, Thomas Edison replied, "I didn't fail 1,000 times. The light bulb was an invention with 1,000 steps." For Edison, failure was not just a piece of the process but a requirement for success. Without the many challenges he faced during the invention process, Edison would not have learned from his mistakes or ultimately brought a commercially viable lightbulb to the world. Unfortunately, companies today tend to downplay failure, deny its occurrence, or experience shame when others recognize it first. Where does this come from? Take adolescent sports, for example. League organizers hand out participation trophies to all the participants rather than embracing the fact that some people win and others lose. What are adolescents learning about failure? By distorting the line between success and failure, these adolescent sports leagues and universities are impeding the development of these young people. Simply put, today's society is coddling future leaders and setting them up for later, more significant, failure by not letting them experience failure early in life.

If people have not experienced failure or have had a bad experience with failure, they will be reluctant to try anything that could result in failure. If employees believe a certain action will deliver a negative result, they will avoid taking that action. If, on the other hand, they believe an action will be positive, it's far easier to move forward with it. Taking action, or not taking action, gives a result of one sort or another. If employees don't like the result they received when they made a decision to act, those results circle right back around to affect their beliefs. More than likely, they won't try again.

Creating a culture of continuous improvement is about creating great workplaces that people love being a part of: a workplace where people are able to use their brainpower and feel supported, included, and respected; a workplace where every action delivers positive results, whether a celebration of a correct decision, or a celebration of something learned by an incorrect decision. Like Edison, people need to believe that failure is a necessary part of success and risk is acceptable to get there.

> **Creating a culture of continuous improvement is about creating great workplaces that people love being a part of.**

The goal of accepting prudent risk is to increase the probability of realizing great reward. Risk is often viewed as negative and something people should avoid, but thoughtful, habitual risk-taking is actually a requirement for high-level success. The only way to garner maximum

> **Do you want to know how to change a culture? Empower your team to make decisions.**

reward in any business process is to promote risk-taking and experimentation by all employees.

Do you want to know how to change a culture? Empower your team to make decisions. Help them define problems accurately. Support them. Stand alongside them. Coach them. Respect them. Create an environment where it's safe to fail. If you do these things, they will follow you anywhere!

Developing An Adaptive Capacity

We discussed this topic earlier in the book, but it's worth revisiting in this chapter. Captain Abrashoff began by setting contingencies, boundaries, and standards to help create consistency and stability for his team. Clear communication around contingencies and boundaries helps support transparency and develop trust, while standards create the short-term stability needed to maintain a chaos-free environment. Once boundaries are set and stability is reached, it's time to begin developing adaptive capacity within each of your team members.

If team members are not given a chance to learn and grow because they are shielded from failure, they remain untested and are more likely to confront difficult future situations in negative ways or not act at all. In other words, these members are not developing what Warren Bennis and Robert J. Thomas refer to as adaptive capacity[*] because they do not have the opportunity to do so. On the other hand, members who develop this capacity and build individual resilience are far more likely to continue trying, and even to promote that behavior among their peers.

In the military, I witnessed many leaders who tried to solve every problem themselves. It became clear very quickly that they would not be able to solve each and every problem themselves; rather, they needed to instill in their personnel an attitude and ability to learn and adapt to an ever-changing environment. Those military leaders needed

---
[*] Warren Bennis and Robert J. Thomas, Crucibles of Leadership, Harvard Business Review, Sept. 2002

to encourage a culture of adaptation coupled with an insatiable drive to win—a culture of innovation.

How Can We Learn As Much As We Can, As Fast As We Can?

In general, people will try anything easy that doesn't work before we will embrace anything harder that does. This thinking is what leads to the repetition of the same problems. We live with short-term countermeasures rather than solving the root cause of the problem. Instead, we need to deal with problems in a robust manner.

Who remembers the scientific method from high school? We learned the scientific method as a process for experimentation, which we could use to explore observations and answer questions.

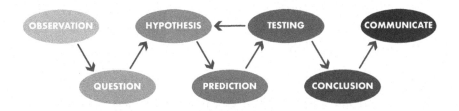

Here is how it works: Let's imagine I walk into my house and I turn on the light switch, but the light in the entryway doesn't come on. My observation is that the light didn't come on. My question is, "Why didn't the light come on?" My hypothesis is, "The light didn't come on because the bulb is burnt out." My prediction is that if I change the light bulb, then the light will work again. So, I test my hypothesis. If I change the bulb and it still doesn't work, then my hypothesis was wrong, and I need a new hypothesis. If the light does work, then I have a conclusion and I can communicate back to my wife that I fixed the light. The scientific method, and scientific thinking, need to become a routine.

By developing a routine, you are creating intentional coordination between what we think will happen and what actually happens. The learning happens as we navigate between these two conditions.

Many people try and fail...try and fail...try and fail...and eventually QUIT.

Scientific thinking is about intentional learning throughout. Scientific thinkers, on the contrary, try, study the failure, learn, adjust...try, study the failure, learn, adjust...SUCCEED.

Case Study: Company Continuous Improvement Vs. Company Continuous Appearance

At Company Continuous Appearance, they liked to say they had a structured problem-solving process. However, Chris and the rest of the leadership team did not drive accountability or inclusion of those closest to where the problem originated. The mid-management team was 100% responsible for identifying and owning problems, from identification to solution.

There were many flaws in this approach. How many problems can one manager attend to? When you pile on all the managers other responsibilities, something has to give. Compare this to all the problems the entire team-member population could contribute to. Imagine how strong the organization would be if everyone was engaged in good root cause analysis and countermeasure implementation. At Company Continuous Appearance, most problems were met with short-term solutions and intentions to go back later to conduct a proper root cause analysis.

Most managers were mandated to complete and submit paperwork showing proper corrective actions. Most of these corrective action reports were completed in twenty minutes by Darrell or Todd sitting alone at their desk. They had intentions of returning, but then never did. Many times, they assumed they knew what the problem was without actually going and seeing the problem. They assumed they knew how to solve the problem, without actually finding the real root cause. They assumed they had fixed the problem, without actually checking to make sure the solutions were doing what they expected.

I was once asked to assist a project team with an ongoing problem, or should I say "problems," at Company Continuous Appearance after multiple missed shipments over a three-week period. Chris and I walked the production floor together. He explained all the problems they were experiencing. It seemed as though everything was hitting at once, he said. He called it the perfect storm. When I started to dig into each of the problems they were experiencing, I found multiple completed corrective actions for the same problems. Further investigation revealed lots of short-term fixes and/or symptom fixes. There were not very many corrective action reports with completed root cause analysis and PDCA activities. Some didn't have any planning while others completely missed the check phase. They had placed band-aids on everything. And now, those band-aids were all popping off at the same time.

I explained to Chris that it was going to take some time to get things in order, but that the proper response was to conduct proper root cause investigations and PDCA activities for each problem. We needed to drive to the root cause and put the proper solutions in place, checking to assure those problems were reduced and/or eliminated permanently. His response was that we didn't have time for that nonsense. He then went on to give me a list of solutions he felt would work best and told me to move ahead in getting them implemented. Needless to say, we created more temporary fixes and increased our fire-fighting efforts over the next few months.

An unstructured problem-solving process like the one at Company Continuous Appearance was far more time-consuming than the structured problem-solving process at Company Continuous Improvement.

Company Continuous Improvement was much more successful because they stepped back and looked at the symptom (what we see), the defect (caused by something), and the root cause (what made it happen). They followed a ten-step method.

Once, we identified a problem with the floor drains at Company Continuous Improvement. Many times, the floor drains would overflow into the production area and no one knew why. In fact, it became such a problem that team members started wearing waders and waterproof boots to work. The first thing we did was to clarify the problem. It took some time, but we set up data collection across the three shifts for when, where, and what time the drains were overflowing.

It wasn't until we started tracking the times and locations that we were able to see a pattern. By properly defining the problem, we were very close to a solution.

We could have listened to the maintenance manager who thought the drains were clogged and needed to be cleaned out. We could have jumped to the conclusion that the team leaders were running too much water when cleaning the machines. But we didn't. We spent the time to properly define the problem using data.

At this point, we pulled together a cross-functional team of maintenance personnel, team leaders, operators, environmental health and safety personnel, a facility manager, and an outside drain expert. We conducted a cause-and-effect exercise with the group based on the information we had already collected, and we landed on a proposed root cause: The plant across the road changed shifts at 5:00 am and 4:00 pm. Prior to changing shifts, they cleaned all their equipment, sending a surge of water and chemicals through the drains. The same drains connected to our plant. At that same time, we were also cleaning our equipment.

We spent the next few days collecting data to verify our root cause. We conducted several experiments in coordination with the neighboring plant and confirmed our hypothesis. We learned more about drains that we wanted to! After identifying and selecting a solution, we were ready to prepare a plan of action. Leadership approved the resource allocation based on the cost savings analysis we delivered along with the proposal and data to back up our selected root cause and solution.

Within two weeks of approval, the problem was rectified, and our team members could go back to wearing their normal work boots. We conducted the proper follow-up checks to assure the problem was eliminated and moved on to our next improvement.

Your Call To Action

Does your organization have a structured problem-solving process in place, and is it being followed? If your desire is to create a learning organization, then you need to develop an organization where your people are able, willing, and excited to experiment. That doesn't mean you open up the floodgates and just allow people to begin doing whatever they want. This will create a wild west mentality with no real direction. There needs to be structure, follow-through, and follow-up: a good PDCA cycle for experiments. One way to develop structure early on is to train your leaders as Kata coaches and adopt Kata storyboards. Choose problems relevant and tied directly to business problems and allow the team to learn together. Allow the team to fail. Make the process visible to management at all levels and create opportunities to involve everyone.

AVOIDING THE CONTINUOUS APPEARANCE TRAP

Answer all questions using the following abbreviations:

1=No 2=Sometimes 3=Mostly 4=Yes/Always

HOW SAFE IS IT FOR YOUR EMPLOYEES TO FAIL?	
1. Do your leaders encourage risk taking?	
2. Do the majority of people experiment with improvements?	
3. Do the majority of people celebrate learning?	
4. Are your leaders creating an environment for team members to grow?	
5. Is your entire team following scientific thinking methodologies?	
QUESTION 9 TOTAL	

Transfer your total to the full assessment at the end of the book. Compare totals to establish a priority.

QUESTION 10

What Is Your High Value Target Area?

> **"Once your problem is clarified, break it down into manageable pieces."**
> ~Lean Enterprise Institute

Desmond Tutu once wisely said that "there is only one way to eat an elephant: a bite at a time." What he meant by this is that everything in life that seems daunting, overwhelming, and even impossible can be accomplished gradually by taking it on just little by little.

Sometimes, in our naivety or arrogance, we try to tackle huge projects that simply swallow us in the size of their scope. Or we think we can turn with the entire cargo ship on a dime. In our workaday world, the reality is that we simply cannot take on the entire organization at once!

In his biography of one of the top Allied leaders in WWII, *Omar Nelson Bradley: America's GI General*[*], historian Steven Assad tells of the enormous problem Bradley took on after the victory in Europe. President Harry S. Truman, who had just taken on the top job after the death of the beloved President Franklin D. Roosevelt, knew he had a disaster in the making with the Veterans Administration (VA). Established to manage a slate of public benefits granted to those who'd

---
[*] Ossad, Steven, *Omar Nelson Bradley: Amerca's GI General, 1893-1981*, University of Missouri (Novemeber 19, 2017)

QUESTION 10

fought in the First World War, it had become mired in bureaucracy and was failing even before the Second World War began. Foreseeing the enormous numbers of newly-minted veterans who would be requiring VA support very soon, Truman asked Bradley to take over the troubled department.

Bradley saw very clearly right up front that trying to fix a bureaucratic mess like that by steamrolling the whole thing at once was an obvious trap and would be doomed to fail. So he took the divide-and-conquer approach. He tackled the long waits that existing veterans were experiencing by launching an aggressive hospital-building program, ensuring that there was a well-distributed network of providers across the nation, located in high-population areas to best serve the greatest numbers of veterans. He addressed the bottlenecks on the administrative side by establishing a number of new leadership and support positions distributed through the country by region, and staffed them with experience logistics experts from his now-dissolved First Army. And he personally attacked the funding problem by using his own popularity to sell the need for investment to the population and to their representatives in Congress, and by having his boss—the President—clear what logjams he found he couldn't plow through himself.

The result was a new, and newly-energized, public service organization that performed marvelously when the hundreds of thousands of veterans returned from Europe and the Pacific. It administered the new GI Bill, a benefit that remains famous even today for the college educations it provided that helped launch the American post-war economic boom.

When we try to take on too much at one time, we get lost, overwhelmed, and frustrated. This is also when executive leaders or managers begin to get impatient and want to move the organization toward another initiative...another flavor of the month. The team begins to run out of energy and time, and leaders either give up too early or hang on too long. The result is failure and disappointment.

AVOIDING THE CONTINUOUS APPEARANCE TRAP

If you have ever tried to take on a big challenge, you know that sometimes it can be difficult to decide how to start. In fact, sometimes challenges are so big that some people get overwhelmed and never even start at all! By choosing one area to begin with, the daunting challenge becomes a lot smaller than originally expected.

> **By choosing one area, the daunting challenge becomes a lot smaller than originally expected.**

It is important that we identify one high-value target value stream or model area to analyze and improve first. This one model area becomes our focus. Once complete, this high-value target area will become our organizational benchmark: the benchmark by which all other improvement initiatives are measured.

In my experience, when a group of people volunteer to participate in a high-value target situation, where the business is exploring organizational transformation, the people who volunteer are often viewed poorly by those who are resistant and perhaps unwilling to participate in the experiment. This is unfortunate; however, as the organization begins to experiment, and the high-value target area begins to gain traction, the organization begins to enjoy success. They see this approach as something better than the historical approach. Many people will start to sign up for these high-value target experiments; in this way, one high-value target area becomes two high-value target areas, and then three and so on, until the organization has developed a high-value target department full of high-value target areas. That department becomes a model for the site and eventually, the site becomes a model for the organization. Over time, more and more people are involved.

Each organization's timeline of implementation for a high-value target value stream is going to be different. Do not get caught up in trying to achieve the same results as other organizations. You are on your own

QUESTION 10

journey. Make it your journey, not someone else's.

Many people adopting a lean methodology believe they have to do everything exactly the same way Toyota did in their Toyota Production System referred to earlier. Their system helped establish many of the foundational practices used by lean practitioners today. However, Toyota developed tools and techniques in response to problems they were having within their organization. These problems might be different than the problems you are having, therefore, may demand for a different response, tool, or technique than those Toyota used. In my experience, this is one area many organizations struggle on their lean journey. They try to adopt Toyota's tools and techniques in the exact manner Toyota deployed them, whether they need them or not.

Don't get me wrong here, Toyota was integral in the establishment of lean methodology and we cannot miss the fact that they were a major player in developing the continuous improvement strategies used around the world today. However, understand that you are not Toyota and it's not about the tools Toyota developed and used. It was the thorough process behind the creation of the tools that you need to learn and apply.

> **It was the thorough process behind the creation of the tools that you need to learn and apply.**

High-value target areas give you a kind of sandbox to experiment and learn. You can prove out your tools and techniques before spreading them to other areas. A high-value target area also offers a way to showcase the hard work your team has put in. On a smaller scale, you can prove out your structured problem-solving process, problem solvers, and the bottom-line results of becoming a learning organization. You can model your leader coaching behavior and the benefits a new management system will provide to the company.

Once you have shown progress and proven out the benefits, it's time to take another bite! This time, the process will be much easier because of the learning from your first high-value target area. Each time, your experience will get a little easier. However, each new high-value target area will also bring its own challenges because every area is different and the people will be different.

One way to reduce the obstacles when replicating learning from one high-value area to another is to use shared resources. Identify leaders who were part of one successful high-value target area and have them take part in the development of a new high-value target area. Sometimes, as teams are able to find more efficient ways to do things, fewer people are needed to complete the same work content. This is a great opportunity to add these people to your team of trailblazing change agents, or to move them to the next high-value target project to share their learning.

Case Study: Company Continuous Improvement vs. Company Continuous Appearance

I was once part of an acquisition at Company Continuous Appearance. We purchased a company with a plant in Arizona, and I was asked to assist with the onboarding. In addition to me, Company Continuous Appearance transferred a seasoned Operations Manager to manage the onboarding process. He had been with the company a long time, and this was offered to him as a potential development and promotional opportunity. I learned later he was also promised an incentive retirement bonus based on the financial impact of the onboarding. We will call him Trevor.

During Trevor's first visit to the production floor, he made changes and gave orders to floor workers without any dialogue or understanding of what the job entailed. Trevor wasn't in the role long before he rolled out his high-level plan, which was more of a total plant transformation than a simple onboarding. He hired an outside consulting company from Boston to come in and complete an analysis of the operation,

QUESTION 10

from financials to process and material flow. They were not on site for more than three weeks before they delivered their results and recommendations. Upon receiving the assessment results, Trevor assigned action items to his management team and the overhaul began.

Trevor's onboarding plan included many changes to the entire plant at once. The plan called for a total redesign of the site, as well as a new material flow plan. The new floor plan called for elimination of some machines, and the movement of the rest from one spot to another. The financial analysis reported overspending in many areas and recommended a freeze on all spending until new procedures were established. The labor report showed their workforce included 10% more than necessary to meet customer needs.

Trevor asked me to facilitate Kaizen events in each work center with a goal to reduce labor and improve flow. I was reluctant to carry out the orders, knowing what would happen; however, I was given no choice. After the first few Kaizen events, we were able to reduce labor needed by ten total people. That next quarter, Trevor announced labor downsizing and forty people lost their jobs. During our next scheduled kaizen event, no one volunteered to take part...and for good reason.

Within a month of Trevor assuming leadership, the plant was in complete chaos. Machine moves were underway, people were scared about losing their jobs, no one could purchase items they needed to do their jobs, and the onboarding was a complete flop. After all these years, I still don't think this plant has recovered. What a mess.

On the other hand, I was also lucky enough to experience an acquisition and plant onboarding at Company Continuous Improvement—and what a difference it was! We spent the first few months getting to know the new team. It was a smaller team, so I was able to sit down one-on-one with each individual and get to know them at a different level. They shared the good, bad, and ugly of past leadership and their decisions, and through the many conversations I was able to gain a clear understanding of the current state of their operation. From here, we established a desired future state. This desired state included Company Continuous Improvement expectations and was combined with the acquired company's leadership team expectations. They were afraid all the work they had put in over the past year would be thrown out. When they realized we respected them enough to listen and combine their past great work with our expectations, the team was fully on board. It was a slow transition at first, but once the team understood we were there to build them up and help, the crawl turned into a walk, and then a run!

In helping the new team make the transition, we were very heavy on change management. One of the techniques we used to engage the new team members and create alignment with our company vision and purpose was to solicit motivational quotes from each individual. We used these quotes on banners with our company logo and vision statement. Each quote was printed with the individual's name on it. While it was a small and inexpensive action, it showed respect, developed trust, and created ownership for the individuals working in the plant. But most of all, it solidified the new partnership, and the new team was proud to be the newest addition to Company Continuous Improvement.

Your Call To Action

When your company is faced with the need for a large, culture-changing transformation, the worst thing you can do is to try to change everything at once. Your responsibility as a lean leader is to make the transition as quickly as you can while ensuring business continuity, and that means understanding up front that the big project will have to be broken down into a number of smaller projects. As with all improvement activities, you should do this with your True North in mind, and involve the workers who will be affected by the changes to take part in each element's planning and execution. Do all of that correctly, and in time you'll find that you and your team have successfully consumed the entire elephant!

QUESTION 10

Answer all questions using the following abbreviations:

1=No 2=Sometimes 3=Mostly 4=Yes/Always

WHAT IS YOUR HIGH VALUE TARGET AREA?	
1. Do the majority of people regularly break larger problems down into smaller problems?	
2. Do the majority of people control and not allow "scope creep?"	
3. Have you chosen one high value target area to experiment with?	
4. Do you have a plan to sustain and replicate learnings to other areas?	
5. Do you already know the next area you are planning to improve?	
QUESTION 10 TOTAL	

Transfer your total to the full assessment at the end of the book. Compare totals to establish a priority.

QUESTION 11

Are You Generating Small, Simple Improvements?

> "**Everybody Engaged Every-day in problem solving and continuous improvement. This creates actions and habits that give people a line of sight to how they're contributing to the company, its true north and business goals."**
>
> ~Tracey Richardson, Coauthor of
> The Toyota Engagement Equation

I'll never forget when I finally had the opportunity to visit the Grand Canyon for the first time. The sheer size of this natural wonder is simply staggering the first time you see it in person.

Over time with persistence, the Colorado River has cut through rock and helped form what we now know as the Grand Canyon. What if we used that same persistence within our organizations? Can you imagine the results you would experience with unwavering, passionate consistency?

It's like that when you're training for a marathon. Trust me, you wouldn't want to simply show up and try to run a marathon without training, or even with spotty or short-term preparation. That would be a disaster. Structured marathon training plans take about eighteen weeks, and that's if you're already running twenty miles a week even before you start the program. If not, it'll take even longer to get ready.

Even if you're starting from a good base, you won't be running super-long distances at the beginning. You'll start with runs from three to eight miles, but you'll be doing them five or six days a week. You may also be throwing in cross-training, perhaps some strength work. You'll mix things up with your running pace, too, with easy days, tempo days, hill sessions, sprints, and even some shorter races.

As the weeks go by, you'll slowly increase your miles. You'll work hard for a few weeks, then take an easier week to recover, because recovery is a critical part of improving. Remember Question 4? Recovery, in this sense, is like allowing time to stabilize between improvements.

Eventually you get to where you're doing near-marathon distances of twenty or more miles. And the amazing thing is that by this point in your training plan, long runs like those aren't even super-difficult; because you've spent the time steadily building your fitness level, you'll find you're readily able to run distances that might have seemed almost impossible when you first dreamed of running a marathon.

Marathon training is a great example of the enormous power of small improvements, with efforts that are sustained over time. And what works for fitness will also work in business.

When I think about small, consistent improvements in the business environment, I cannot help but reflect on Paul Akers and Fastcap. Paul does an amazing job communicating the simplicity of lean. However, if you know anything about Paul, you know his unwavering persistence and passion for small improvements. Yes, it's simple, but simple does not mean easy. As the CEO of Fastcap, Paul arrives to work early with a relentless drive for continuous improvement in the small things, on a daily basis. He doesn't start his day in the office; rather, he is out talking to everyone, asking them to show him their improvements. He makes videos and shows them to the entire team, celebrating every single improvement loudly and visibly, no matter how small, every single day.

Develop your learning organization with small improvements by engaging the minds of your team. Here is the recipe:

Recipe:

Ingredients:
- Ask for simple ideas daily.
- Implement ideas with help from your team daily.
- Celebrate success daily.

Simple, right? Don't let complexity slow you down. Just start.

You must be careful, however, that your improvements are aligned with your True North and tied to actionable metrics. In his book *Measures of Success*[*], Mark Graban says, "What's easy to measure isn't always what's meaningful to our business." He mentions the dangers of vanity metrics and how they can place attention in the wrong area. He goes on to say, "Instead of looking at the things that paint a picture of success, we should look at metrics that are truly our KPIs for our organization."

Consider the Impact/Effort Matrix introduced in Question 3. When it

---
[*] Mark Graban, Measures of Success (US: Constancy Inc., 2019)

comes to continuous improvement, you must consider your return on investment. "Investment" falls under "Effort" in this matrix. Effort or Investment could encompass a few categories; we could refer to people resources, financial resources, or time investment. The "Return" or Impact of the solutions could also be financial or could also include freed up time and resources. For small improvements, the investment, or effort is often very small and the net ROI is much, much higher!

Are You Celebrating Success on Small Wins?

> *"Great things are done by a series of small things brought together."* ~Vincent Van Gogh

One of the main reasons employees leave their jobs is that they don't feel appreciated, yet some reports show that a large percentage of employees, usually over 65%, haven't received any form of recognition over the past year.

Organizations should be committed to celebrating success. Leaders should find ways to add energy to their team, to motivate others to do kaizen just as they do themselves. They can do this by complimenting team members for personal performance and by handing out small rewards for every improvement made. Both public and private recognition is important. Find every opportunity to communicate the amazing things happening around your company.

Are You Sharing Your Wins?

> *"Lean isn't lean if it doesn't involve everyone."*
> ~John Shook

As humans, our feelings of self-esteem and self-confidence rest on being able to take pride in our achievements. I would go as far as to say it's healthy to brag about yourself, in the right context. Giving your team the ability to boast and get a pat-on-the-back for a job well done can help boost confidence and prepare your team for future successes.

Growing up, most of us were told never to boast. However, when it comes to continuous improvement, we want employees to share and celebrate every accomplishment. By sharing wins, we are reinforcing the actions we want to see from our teams. Reinforcement is probably the most important step in ensuring a successful change. As the saying goes, success breeds success.

Case Study: Company Continuous Improvement vs. Company Continuous Appearance

Company Continuous Appearance was focused on vanity metrics rather than actionable metrics. For example, they measured and celebrated the number of Six Sigma Green Belts and Black Belts trained and certified each year. They went further to track the number of completed improvements and projects. These metrics caused the organization to focus in the wrong area. Managers with the most certified belts under their command completing the most projects were promoted, while managers truly improving their business through those few properly focused projects, generating the right actions and results, were passed over.

The company had lots of trained belts, but no real results. Improvement activities were scattered and followed no structured plan. There were a lot of simple ideas, but they were not necessarily meaningful to the business.

Company Continuous Improvement, on the other hand, focused on leading and on actionable measures. All improvement activities followed a structured plan and were measured by metrics relatable to those people working in the business. They knew how their work and improvement activities would truly impact the business.

For example, at the plant level, safety was measured by lost workday injuries. However, lost workday injuries is a lagging measure and Company Continuous Improvement knew this. The team determined that an actionable metric of near-miss injuries was a better leading measure. From here, they adopted a kind of behavior-based safety program intended to focus workers' attention on their own and their peers' daily safety behavior. Without the proper culture, this program may not have been successful. Company Continuous Appearance mandated safety observations and tried to force safe behavior on their employees. Company Continuous Improvement, rather, helped their employees to see the value of change beginning with small improvements. In order to create belief in the change, improving safety behaviors had to be practiced. In addition to the focus on team member behaviors, corporate management supported and encouraged safe behavior by eliminating root causes through structured problem solving. Some of these root causes included engineering, process, and communication or training failures.

These new actions were supported and reinforced through acknowledgment, celebration, and support from leadership and from the whole team. Proactive behavior coupled with the measurement of near-miss accidents, and followed by small improvements generated through structured problem solving, resulted in an amazing safety-based culture and, ultimately, a reduction of lost work day injuries.

Your Call To Action

Have you created a structure and environment for small, simple improvements to be generated and celebrated? How do you know where to start? In keeping our focus on the improvement kata model, you must know what your desired state or target condition is before you begin. The kata methodology can then bring the structure you need to your improvement activities.

Do not ask yourself, "What *can* I improve?" There are hundreds of thousands of things you *can* improve. This question gives no direction. Rather, you must ask yourself, "What do I *need* to improve?" This question brings light to your target condition. Once you know your target condition and you know where you are, you now have direction. There will be many problems, initiatives, and unknown activities that will try to pull you off your path. You do not know all the challenges you will face on your path toward your target condition. You must commit yourself and your team to small, rapid experiments to advance your knowledge quickly, moving you away from what isn't working to what is working.

Small, simple improvements should be made through experimentation toward your target condition. This practice must be consistent and deliberate.

QUESTION 11

Answer all questions using the following abbreviations:

1=No 2=Sometimes 3=Mostly 4=Yes/Always

ARE YOU GENERATING SMALL, SIMPLE IMPROVEMENTS?	
1. Are you asking for simple improvements daily?	
2. Are you implementing small, simple improvements daily?	
3. Are you celebrating improvements daily?	
4. Do you have a way to share your wins with other areas?	
5. Do you recognize team members and show them appreciation?	
QUESTION 11 TOTAL	

Transfer your total to the full assessment at the end of the book. Compare totals to establish a priority.

QUESTION 12

Are Problems Easy To See?

> **"Having no problem is the biggest problem of all"**
>
> ~Taiichi Ohno, Engineer and Manager at the Toyota Production Company

Have you ever noticed how often sports fans glance up at the scoreboard? Why would people do that when all the action is on the field? Well, it's not too hard to figure out why the scoreboard gets so much interest. It answers all the questions we have about the status of the game. What's the score? How much time is left?

How does this relate if we compare the scoreboard to your organization? Can you tell how you are doing at a glance? Where are you in relation to your goal? Your goals are like the score in the game. How have you been performing hour by hour? Perhaps that's your innings, or quarters. Do you need to switch players? Maybe you need to adjust your labor to reach your goal. Just like a sporting event, we need real-time, up-to-date information and feedback.

Problems should be made easy to see with your eyes. If done correctly, we should be able to see at a glance how we're doing without having to read through reports, look up data on a computer, or wait for someone to brief us on our status. How many problems could you begin to

QUESTION 12

address if you had only known there was a problem?

By making problems visible, we provide teams with the information they need. This is a fundamental part of empowerment and ownership, and can help them to reduce waste and poor quality. This information needs to be current and in real time. Having good data presented to the team takes away the excuse of, "I didn't know we had a problem." If we provide teams with feedback, give them responsibility, and hold them accountable for their actions, they will become more efficient by reducing response time. If we get the information out of the computer, and in front of the team that needs to see it, we will be taking great steps to becoming a transparent organization.

The beauty of making problems visible is we all have years of experience doing it. Let's look at some of the ways we make problems visible every day. Using "best by" dates on our food can prevent us from making some bad choices. Think about the milk in your refrigerator. If your milk is far out of date, you certainly don't want to drink it. Nothing a trip to the grocery store can't fix. You might drive to the store in your car, where the symbols on your dash are there to warn you of existing or potential problems.

Once at the store the meat, dairy, bakery, and deli departments are advertised up high, in large letters, so you know immediately where to go. Now that you found the milk, it's time to check out. Faced with seemingly endless checkout lanes you use visuals once again. What lanes are lighted, indicating they are open? Now that you found someone to ring you up you might have to press the green key indicating the amount you are getting charged is correct.

AVOIDING THE CONTINUOUS APPEARANCE TRAP

How can we make problems visible within your organization? You undoubtedly have a level of visuals already in place for such things as exits, fire extinguishers, and clearance around electrical panels. These visuals are required by law for your safety, but what about the not-so-obvious ones? Do you have others? Are you missing out on the benefits of making problems visible?

The power in visual management is its ability to bridge the language and cultural gaps that naturally exist in today's world. The information needs to be complete enough to enable us, with just one glance, to make the right decisions. A message communicated through a simple picture is quick, clear, and easily understood.

In the place where the value-add work is being done, the presence of visual controls quickly lets us know where we are standing. When we, as visitors to a company, can understand what is going on around us, without being told, the visual tools in place are accomplishing their task. Some things should never be left to chance; evacuation routes and fire or medical symbols should be the first place you begin if you are introducing visual management to your organization. What's next?

Identifying problems quickly is our best chance to limit the negative effects they can have on our organization. If we use visual controls correctly, we can become better problem solvers. We can't fix what we don't know. If we can identify abnormalities quickly, we can begin to correct them without delay.

Problems can arise when we need to get our message out there but find ourselves faced with different languages, age groups, and cultures. How do we translate our message to everybody? Visual instructions may or may not include text, but since everyone learns differently, it's a good idea to have both text and pictures; consider video, digital, or other technical solutions as well. Visual instructions are meant to explain a process. Whether it's experienced operators, new hires using your instructions, or a traveler in a different country, a text-first approach is not very effective. A better way is to include pictures, symbols, or graphics, showing how the process works, what something looks like, or something to avoid. Using pictures also reduces the need to print various instructions in different languages.

Visual measurements are not as simple as posting a pretty chart on the wall. You need to determine the audience that needs to see the data. Will this

> A better way is to include pictures, symbols, or graphics, showing how the process works, what something looks like, or something to avoid.

be hourly production metrics for operators trying to stay on track? Perhaps you want to display each day without injury at your daily stand-up meeting. Put yourself in the position of the person receiving the data. Should you use a pie chart or bar graph? Pivot table or Pareto? Maybe a simple line chart, or a gauge indicator that can point to different colors, will do the trick. Remember that the time it takes someone to look at and understand your data, or the distance away from it they will be, are factors that should be taken into account when deciding what format to use. Keep it simple!

Case Study: Company Continuous Improvement Vs. Company Continuous Appearance

Everything was made visual at Company Continuous Improvement. One area of the manufacturing plant was blocked off to create an area we called the Boardwalk. (Some called it the Townhall.) We would hold our daily run-the-business stand-up meetings at the Boardwalk. The company called these visual run-the-business meetings for a reason.

We were very strategic in choosing the location of the Boardwalk. We wanted it to be visible to all team members. We chose to locate the Boardwalk just outside the breakroom doors, where team members would walk past multiple times a day.

The Boardwalk had a total of seven boards on the front: Safety, Quality, Productivity, Inventory, Value Stream Tracking Center 1, Value Stream Tracking Center 2, and Value Stream Tracking Center 3. Located on the back side were a Layered Audit Board and an Idea Tracking Board.

When the magnetic whiteboards arrived, we built our own stands, always on wheels and low enough to allow for a line-of-sight across the tops of the boards, but high enough for ergonomic considerations.

Creating a clear and visible line-of-sight across the tops of the boards was important for a few key reasons. First, the supervisors attending the daily meetings needed the ability to keep their eyes on their areas. Second, a clear line-of-sight across the plant allowed operators to see upstream and downstream of their process; this was helpful in identifying abnormal conditions. We didn't want the Boardwalk to impede line of sight across the plant. Finally, we were creating a transparent culture—a culture with trust and inclusion. We wanted everyone to see and hear what was happening every day inside the Boardwalk. We also invited team members from surrounding areas to join us, as they were able, to listen to and engage in the activities.

Red and green colors were used to quickly identify abnormal conditions inside the Boardwalk. Presenting reality was important to this team, and making problems visible was an important part of presenting reality. Red and green magnets and markers were used on the boards. Red and green slides were used for the layered audit board. Red and green Solo cups were used atop each value stream tracking to show overall value stream status by the hour.

"Why not yellow?," you may be thinking. This team decided yellow was a color that needed to be earned. Many times, companies use yellow as an easy way to get by: We aren't meeting our goals, but we are scared to show that we are in the red, so we will just be yellow. That's safe, right?

At Company Continuous Appearance, people did not feel safe. You would never see red on any chart or board because it wasn't safe to show red. Therefore, everything was green or yellow...never red, even if it should have been red. In fact, at one point, after much discussion, Chris and I decided to take it upon ourselves to create visual boards on the production floor to track safety, quality, cost, delivery, and morale. The boards were textbook: They contained every element necessary for success, including real data. When an executive director was touring the plant, he saw the boards, including the red on some of the charts, and made the following comment, "What do these boards tell you except that your team is underperforming? Take these down before our customers see them, and stick to the same reports we have used in the past." All the boards were removed, and Chris went back to sitting in meetings and listening to report, after report, after report. Some team members were frustrated, while others just put their hands in the air, laughed, and said, "I told you so."

Your Call To Action

Identify those visuals you are already using. Begin experimenting with other visual management inside your organization. As problems are identified, ask yourself how you could create visuals that would make problems visible all the time.

Can someone walk through your facility and identify problems?

AVOIDING THE CONTINUOUS APPEARANCE TRAP

Consider taking time for your own walk-about asking yourself some simple questions: When a red light is blinking over a machine, what is the response to that light? How do team members know they had a successful month? Week? Day? Hour? Can you see defects? What is the response when a defect happens? Ensure you are not missing out on the benefits of making problems visible.

QUESTION 12

Answer all questions using the following abbreviations:

1=No 2=Sometimes 3=Mostly 4=Yes/Always

ARE PROBLEMS EASY TO SEE?	
1. Are you actively seeking ways to make problems visible?	
2. Can you identify problems in your workplace without someone showing you where they are?	
3. Do your visuals translate to everyone?	
4. Do you use simple measurements and are they easy to interpret?	
5. Can you see how your team is responding to problems easily?	
QUESTION 12 TOTAL	

Transfer your total to the full assessment at the end of the book. Compare totals to establish a priority.

Conclusion

AVOIDING THE CONTINUOUS APPEARANCE TRAP

> "From the little spark may burst a mighty flame."
>
> ~Dante Alighieri, Italian Poet and Philosopher

As a volunteer trail leader for teenagers backpacking in Northern Michigan, I have spent many summers teaching the art of fire starting, much of which I learned while serving in the United States Marine Corps. When kids are first asked to build a fire, without any instruction, they normally begin by collecting and stacking large logs and thick sticks in a pile. Using a pocket lighter or igniter, they hold the flame under a thick piece of firewood hoping the flame will spread and start the fire. However, this approach is never effective.

There are many ways to start a fire. However, there are three ingredients that are always necessary: fuel, oxygen, and heat. When one component is absent, the fire goes out. There are also three types of fuel needed to ignite and keep a fire lit. The order of adding these types of fuel is very important. You must add your tinder—for example, wood shavings or lint—to get the fire started. Next, you can add your kindling—small branches or twigs. Finally, you can add your firewood. When following this proven approach, anyone can ignite a fire with even the smallest spark.

CONCLUSION

Just like starting a fire in the forest, there are ingredients necessary to fuel a mighty flame of continuous improvement in any organization. Many times, I see leaders adding "fuel" in the wrong order, or missing certain ingredients, resulting in a smoldering mess. We can stack firewood and create a great looking outer structure, but without tinder or kindling, the fire will never really start or take off into a mighty flame. If I try to

> **Just like starting a fire in the forest, there are ingredients necessary to fuel a mighty flame of continuous improvement in any organization.**

enable action or deploy tools, techniques, or proven solutions before I have set the expectation, then the fire will not burn. If I try to empower my single team for success with no long-term vision or connection to mission, then I will surely fail.

Use the 12-question assessment identified in this book to determine priority and establish the right order for your experiments. Be sure you use all the right ingredients and apply them in the right order that fits for your organization.

Let's identify the tinder, kindling, and firewood needed to build a mighty flame of continuous improvement: first, the tinder. The tinder includes everything involved in setting the proper expectations up front. Once expectations are set, it's time to add the kindling. At this stage we are enabling action within our teams. Finally, it's time to add the firewood. The firewood is long term stability and sustainment of the change. The details behind each of these types of fuel can only be identified through scientific thinking.

Scientific thinking will result in the firewood needed to keep the fire burning. Small, simple improvements are much easier to repeat than larger, complex improvements. Lean culture change requires continuous and frequent touches between people and processes. Although these touches can have different purposes, small improvements every day with frequent touches from leaders can have a huge impact. This is usually simple in practice, only taking a few minutes, but is nevertheless hard work, because it requires an enormous amount of diligence and, sometimes, a little bravery to have uncomfortable conversations.

> **Small, simple improvements are much easier to repeat than larger, complex improvements.**

***

The spread of a continuous improvement culture cannot be confined to your high-value target area. It must be unleashed on the rest of the organization. In fact, if you are doing things right, the culture will begin to spread to other areas of the organization like wildfire.

Inevitably, things will crop up that cause you, your team, and your organization to feel stuck and possibly lose momentum. Do not allow these times to cause loss of sight on your True North. Stay focused and stay the course!

In my travels around the world, I have spent time in many airports. There have been times where my flights were delayed, causing shorter-than-expected connection times. I remember a time when my plane arrived at a connection airport and I had about five minutes to make it from gate A1 to Z99—or at least it seemed that way. At this point, I had three choices. First, I could simply miss my flight. Second, I could call upon one of those golf cart vehicles to move me through the airport. The third choice was to run as fast as I could through the airport and make my connection. While grabbing my carry-on from above my seat, I decided on the third choice. And just as I stepped off the plane, I was on an all-out sprint across the airport. While running, I noticed

CONCLUSION

there were others in the airport who had made the same choice. By the time I passed gates M and N, sweat was running down my face and my arm was ready to fall off from pulling my bag behind me. Then, I saw something I will never forget. Everything inside me jumped for joy! It was a moving walkway. In fact, I could see these moving walkways run all the way down the middle of the airport. Could it be that I could actually make my flight?

As I entered the moving walkway, still on a sprint, I noticed a blockage up ahead. There were others who had stopped and were patiently waiting to move through the blockage. I, too, had to stop. In the first ten seconds of standing still on that moving walkway, I was calculating the lost time and contemplating jumping the barrier. In my mind, since moving walkways move more slowly than a natural walking pace, the only way to fully utilize a moving walkway to make my flight is to run at full speed. But even though my frustrations were high, I stayed and waited to get through the jam. Within a few minutes, I discovered what had been causing the blockage. Two individuals, both holding two very large suitcases (that should have been checked), were standing still in the middle of the moving walkway. People had to push their way past the two individuals. And no matter how politely or not politely they asked, the two individuals were not moving. Of course, I was quite frustrated.

Ultimately, I was able to get through the jam and make my flight that day. But this experience left me with a vivid example of what happens as a continuous improvement culture begins to spread throughout your organization. Those individuals in your high-value target area have stepped onto the moving walkway and are ready to move forward at a fast pace. They have a vision for where they are going and see the path to get there. However, there are still individuals who are stuck. Like those on a moving walkway in an airport, maybe they feel like they are moving forward toward the vision. Maybe they want to *appear* as though they are moving forward. But in fact, they are just standing still—and sometimes, they are moving much more slowly than those around them. This can create high levels of frustration for those who are ready to move forward at a fast pace. If we aren't careful, these frustrations can lead to significant struggles. We do need to respect those that need more time to adapt to change and those who are stuck. However, how do we best support and deploy the spread of a continuous improvement culture given these challenges?

First, you need to commit to doing things a new way. The new way of doing things should be so apparent, so talked about, so actionable, and so ubiquitous that people begin to believe that that is the way things work around your organization. To achieve a culture of continuous improvement, you must be committed to continuous improvement. It must be something that has a focus. It must have equal status to the sales dollars last month, customer service cost, and cost metrics. You must begin to talk about continuous improvement in the same way that you talk about all these other metrics. This is a requirement for all managers. It cannot be something kicked off by the plant manager, CEO, or COO and then left to permeate throughout the organization on its own. If you are the one who is going to kick off this new way of doing things, then you must keep talking about it. It must be a topic of conversation at every meeting, during every walk-about, in every coaching session. This must also be replicated at every layer throughout the organization. Each manager must adopt and deliver the same message continuously as you are. In fact, they must increase the visibility of this message with their teams. For front-line staff, if they have a suggestion or an idea for improvement over some broken process, and the manager just shrugs or says, "Okay, thanks," and does nothing about it, then all the talk coming from executive leadership will be meaningless.

> It must have equal status to the sales dollars last month, customer service cost, and cost metrics.

CONCLUSION

The critical mass of your organization is not in executive leadership. You must get your critical mass to agree and believe in the new way of doing things. They must live it day in and day out for a culture of continuous improvement to take hold. You will need most of your organization committed to this new culture for it to spread. You need at least 50% of the people in the organization who look at what they are doing and think to themselves, "Is there a better way I can do this?"

You might feel stuck at times, but with some intentional experimentation and dedication to learning, and a focus on your True North, you can stay the course!

***

Before I end this book, I want to close with a reminder to you. You can put in a lot of effort to create the perfect long-term goal and strategy around developing the right culture; however, your effort may or may not result in the conclusion you were hoping for. As culture emerges, you cannot place KPIs to it. Rather, you can nudge it in a direction by using experiments as mentioned throughout this book.

In using the questions laid out for you in this book, do not assess your organization or leadership based on how you have already decided to act. While I have given you some suggestions and examples in each of the case studies, you must know these were learned over time and in response to experiments in a certain industry and with a certain team. Your area of business, team, and environment will be much different. When asking yourself each one of these questions, try to prevent yourself from having any knowledge of action. When you have learned enough and are confident to move ahead with action, you must still be careful. It's never a good idea to change an entire culture at once. You must take small steps and pay attention to the results of your efforts along the way.

BJ Fogg, author and social scientist at Stanford University, started doing two push-ups after every bathroom break, identifying the flush of the toilet as his trigger for doing so. In addition to helping him lose weight, this strategy helped him kickstart over one hundred other little positive changes throughout his day. Fogg ended up publishing a book, *Tiny Habits*[*], to showcase how people create routines and successfully form new habits. These tiny habits are Fogg's small steps that eventually led to a total transformation.

Challenge yourself to move toward your long-term vision of total organizational transformation. You can start by putting your answer for each of the questions from this book into action. Do not go after every question at the same time; rather, approach each one as a small step toward your end goal.

As you begin your journey, take time to assess your culture. To really understand what's truly underneath your culture, you need to study your culture, learn, and watch it spread!

At the end of each chapter, you have been given a *Call To Action* and *Chapter Assessment Questions* to help determine your desired state and your current state. As I mentioned in the introduction, this is your challenge. Use the total assessment as a guide to help you determine where to begin. Once you have determined your one question to start with, and you have established the gap between current and desired state for that one question, it's time to conduct experiments, remove obstacles, and begin the journey toward your desired state.

The journey is not easy. Put in the hard work, be consistent and intentional, and above all else, do not give up.

Keep learning and keep moving forward toward your desired state!

And remember...

Keep it Simple. Keep It Visual. And Continue to Improve.

---

[*] Fogg, B. J.. 2020. Tiny Habits: The Small Changes That Change Everything. Boston: Houghton Mifflin Harcourt.

Assessment Questions

Answer all questions using the following abbreviations:

1=No 2=Sometimes 3=Mostly 4=Yes/Always

ARE YOU CONTENT?	
1. Do you communicate a compelling story and vision for growth?	
2. Are you putting out new and innovative products or services?	
3. Are teams discussing improvements?	
4. Are methods and processes being improved?	
5. Is someone assessing the competition and suggesting improvements?	
QUESTION 1 TOTAL	

HOW ARE YOUR LEADERS SPENDING THEIR TIME?	
1. Do team and mid-level leaders spend the majority of their time where the value-add work is being done?	
2. Do executive leaders spend some time where the value-add work is being done?	
3. Do leaders have some type of leader standard work?	
4. Is the right percentage of each leaders work standardized?	
5. Do leaders discuss and make improvements to time-management?	
QUESTION 2 TOTAL	

ARE YOU PURSUING PERFECTION?	
1. Does your organization have a long term vision?	
2. Does everyone know the long term vision?	
3. Do people know how their work personally contributes to the vision?	

ASSESSMENT

4. Is the vision message consistent?	
5. Do you have a formal marketing campaign to communicate your vision?	
QUESTION 3 TOTAL	

HOW STABLE ARE YOU TODAY?

1. Is there stability in your leadership team?	
2. Is your leadership communicating a stable message?	
3. Are you using standardization to sustain improvement gains?	
4. Do you have standard work displayed visually?	
5. Are you updating your standard work as improvements are made?	
QUESTION 4 TOTAL	

WHO'S ACCOUNTABLE?

1. Do you focus on the process and not on blaming people?	
2. Are team members given clear priorities, expectations, and support?	
3. Do leaders follow through with providing proper support to team members?	
4. Do leaders and members share accountability?	
5. Is accountability discussed and communicated throughout the organization regularly?	
QUESTION 5 TOTAL	

WHAT ARE YOUR GOALS?

1. Do your leaders have a 'flexibility of mind'? Do they plan for and anticipate change?	
2. Are you using SMART Goals?	

3. Does your organization have long term and 1-year goals? Are they aligned?	
4. Are you operating on 90-day or similar goal setting cycles?	
5. Are your short goal setting cycles (tactical plan) aligned with your long-term goals?	
	QUESTION 6 TOTAL

IS YOUR ORGANIZATION DESIGNED TO MEET YOUR GOALS?

1. Is your organization designed to share information, goals, priorities, and processes?	
2. Do the majority of people operate with a big picture (value stream) mindset?	
3. Do you identify customer requirements and discuss how to meet demand regularly?	
4. Do the majority of people view your organization or parts of your organization in process steps?	
5. Are you analyzing process steps and/or are you conducting value stream mapping analysis?	
	QUESTION 7 TOTAL

HOW ARE YOUR LEADERS BEHAVING?

1. Is your leadership team engaged?	
2. Are your leaders acting as leaders and managers?	
3. Do your leaders have a formal self-development plan in place?	

ASSESSMENT

4. Are your leaders spending a large amount of time coaching and developing others?	
5. Are all leaders involved in vision casting and goal alignment?	
QUESTION 8 TOTAL	

HOW SAFE IS IT FOR YOUR EMPLOYEES TO FAIL?

1. Do your leaders encourage risk taking?	
2. Do the majority of people experiment with improvements?	
3. Do the majority of people celebrate learning?	
4. Are your leaders creating an environment for team members to grow?	
5. Is your entire team following scientific thinking methodologies?	
QUESTION 9 TOTAL	

WHAT IS YOUR HIGH VALUE TARGET AREA?

1. Do the majority of people regularly break larger problems down into smaller problems?	
2. Do the majority of people control and not allow "scope creep?"	
3. Have you chosen one high value target area to experiment with?	
4. Do you have a plan to sustain and replicate learnings to other areas?	
5. Do you already know the next area you are planning to improve?	
QUESTION 10 TOTAL	

ARE YOU GENERATING SMALL, SIMPLE IMPROVEMENTS?

1. Are you asking for simple improvements daily?	
2. Are you implementing small, simple improvements daily?	

3. Are you celebrating improvements daily?	
4. Do you have a way to share your wins with other areas?	
5. Do you recognize team members and show them appreciation?	
QUESTION 11 TOTAL	

ARE PROBLEMS EASY TO SEE?

1. Are you actively seeking ways to make problems visible?	
2. Can you identify problems in your workplace without someone showing you where they are?	
3. Do your visuals translate to everyone?	
4. Do you use simple measurements and are they easy to interpret?	
5. Can you see how your team is responding to problems easily?	
QUESTION 12 TOTAL	
ASSESSMENT TOTAL	

Use the totals from each section to determine where to start. Your lowest scores should become a priority for you. Now add up all 12 sections and place your total assessment score above. Anything less than 120 should create significant concern. Organizations should establish an initial target condition to fall between 121 and 180. However, organizations should set a long term direction or challenge to be above 210.

About The Author

Patrick is an internationally recognized leadership coach, consultant, and professional speaker, best known for his unique human approach to sound team-building practices, creating consensus and enabling empowerment. He founded his consulting practice in 2018 to work with leaders at all levels and organizations of all sizes to achieve higher levels of performance. He motivates, inspires, and drives the right results at all points in business processes.

Patrick has been delivering bottom-line results through specialized process improvement solutions for over twenty years. He's worked with all types of businesses from private, non-profit, government, and manufacturing ranging from small business to billion-dollar corporations.

Patrick holds a BS with honors from Eastern Michigan University and a Master of Business Administration. Patrick lives in the West Michigan Area with his wife and his three children. Patrick also founded a non-profit organization back in 2005 that helps empower and equip at-risk

ABOUT THE AUTHOR

youth for positive change. His company volunteers and donates a portion of their proceeds to help with scholarships. Learn more about this charity at www.remembranceranch.org.

Learn more at:

www.findleansolutions.com | www.avoidcontinuousappearance.com

GO BEYOND THE BOOK

Are you inspired by the messages and key learnings found within Avoiding the Continuous Appearance Trap? Go beyond the book and engage Patrick Adams to meet the needs of your organization and your team. From delivering custom learning experiences such as keynote addresses to interactive workshops to empowering your leaders with coaching, count on Patrick to provide your business improvement solutions.

Get in Contact:

office@findleansolutions.com

Find, Follow, and Share on Social Media:

@PatrickAdamsii

@FindingLeanSolutions

@pa.consulting